ISBN: 9798414729969

Tennis Teaching: Art or Science?

A Modern Guide for Tennis Teachers and Coaches

John R Williams

About the Author:

Photo: The author with his wife Joyce at the Breakers Hotel in Palm Beach, FL

John Williams is a widely acclaimed coach, tennis teaching professional and author of the best-selling book , *A Modern Guide for Tennis Improvement.* He has been a United States Professional Tennis Association (USPTA) member since 1972. John says enthusiastically "I enjoy interacting with people and teaching them the wonderful game of tennis."

John has a bachelor's degree in math and physics from the University of Charleston, a master's degree in astrophysics from Florida State University, and has completed three years of doctoral study in nuclear physics at Auburn University. John is currently a retired professor of Physics and Astronomy at St. Petersburg College in Clearwater, FL.

,

John served as president and regional vice president for the Missouri Valley Professional Tennis Association (MVPTA) from 1983-1991, vice president of the Florida Professional Tennis Association (FPTA) from 1978-1981, and regional vice president for the Mid-Atlantic Professional Tennis Association (MAPTA) from 1973-1975. John was inducted into the University of Charleston Hall of Fame in 2001 and the Missouri Valley Professional Tennis Association (MVPTA) Hall of Fame in 1999. He was named the Pinellas County Florida Coach of the Year in 1977 and 1981, and his family was named the Oklahoma Tennis Family of the Year in 1996 and 1999.

Previous places of employment include Oakwood Country Club in Enid, OK, McMullen Tennis Complex in Clearwater, FL, and Cross Keys Tennis Club in Baltimore, MD. He has coached and developed players of all ages and abilities. They include state, sectional and national champions in multiple locales from Florida to Oklahoma. Even though he is appreciative of his industry accolades, John says, "My wife and children are my pride and joy."

As a player, John was a nationally ranked junior from 1958-1961. He was the number one ranked player at the University of Charleston from 1961-1965, and a three-time All-American. He lost only one regular season match in four years. John also played professionally and held a top 50 USA ranking from 1965-1969. John has given exhibitions and clinics all over the United States and the Caribbean. Most noteworthy of these was a 1974 exhibition and clinic with Stan Smith in Baltimore, MD (Stan was the 1972 world number one and Wimbledon champion).

About the Book:

This book is written for **tennis professionals** and for those who might want to enter the field of **tennis teaching** and become a **professional instructor or coach**. **Parents** who want the best available instruction for their children will find this book essential for selecting the right instructor to help their child fulfill their tennis dreams and to enjoy this great game of tennis for a lifetime. If you are currently a tennis pro and not a member of a professional organization, I strongly recommend that you join either the United States Professional Tennis Association (USPTA) or the Professional Tennis Registry (PTR). [1] The USPTA is the oldest and largest organization of tennis-teaching professionals. It was established in 1927 and offers a platform for the exchange of ideas and for improving the teaching skills and business knowledge of all members. The PTR was founded by Dennis Van der Meer, who was a leading innovator in the field of tennis teaching. Founded in 1976, the PTR certifies tennis teachers and coaches with a goal of growing the game.

Other worth-while organizations that should be considered are the United States Tennis Association (USTA) and the United States Racquet Stringers Association (USRSA). The USTA manages the world's largest annual sporting event: the US Open. The USTA was established in 1881 and strives to grow the game at every level. The USRSA was founded in 1975 and their mission is to educate tennis professionals and retailers to better understand the latest in strings, racquets and stringing machines. As of this writing, the USRSA had over 7,000 members.

In His Own Words:

I played high school tennis at Charleston High School in WV, was their number one player my senior year and a nationally ranked junior in the 18 and under division. My first experience at playing a world class talent occurred when I was 17. I played Arthur Ashe in the Mid-Atlantic Sectional junior tournament in Wheeling, WV. Arthur and I were the same age. Although Arthur beat me in straight sets, it was a great learning experience and only fueled my desire to improve. I continued to develop my tennis skills at Morris Harvey College (now the University of Charleston) and played the number one singles and doubles positions for four years.

Taking an occasional time out during a 35 year tennis-teaching career, I was able to play pro level tournaments in the days of "sham amateurism" (before open tennis) and continued to play and win pro level tournaments (after 1968) until I was 40 years old. I was a 3-time West Virginia Champion, a two-time Ohio Valley Champion, a two-time Maryland State Champion and a two-time Western Maryland Champion. I won the West Virginia Open Doubles Championship 5 times and in 1973 won the Eastern Pro Singles Championship in Woodbury, NY along with a $1000 purse, (It seemed like a lot of money at the time).

Table of Contents

Chapter

Chapter 1
Art or Science?

The ideal tennis teacher is an **artist** making use of current **science.** If teaching were strictly a science, we would have more great tennis teachers in the world. As a tennis teacher, we must realize that every student is unlike any other. Different ages, genders and abilities pose distinct challenges for every instructor. If we use the analogy of an artist creating an original work of art on a blank canvas, we have a picture of what that first meeting with a new student is like. Unlike the artist contemplating the blank canvas, a great teacher realizes that teaching tennis is a two-way street. Feed-back is of utmost importance when teaching tennis to a student or a group. The artist who stares at his blank canvas does not expect feedback from his canvas, pen, or paint. An artist during the creative phase expects no feedback from the tools that are creating the hoped-for masterpiece. Only when the blank canvas is completed, can the artist expect feedback. This assessment from admirers and critics is done only after the canvas is finished. A tennis teacher can observe reactions while teaching the first lesson and each and every lesson thereafter. This constant feedback allows the tennis teacher to adjust his or her teaching methods in the moment. This is the creative portion of the teaching process and is the challenge that every great instructor has as they begin to teach this fantastic game of tennis to a brand-new student.

What about the Science? High speed cameras and slow motion videos have revealed much about how the top professional players hit a tennis ball. The biomechanics and the physics involved in producing the most efficient and most effective swings have been explored, analyzed and recorded. A professional teacher who has played high level tennis has his or her personal store of knowledge on the best way to swing at a tennis ball. Taking this body of science plus the instructors own playing experience is often used as a model to promote improvement through **technique** changes or adjustments. However, an over-focus on **technique** can often yield not only minimal results, but can sometimes cause frustration and injury. Therefore a great instructor should be **an artist** that uses the current **science** to produce the desired outcome (**improvement**).

When you first meet a new student, setting the **proper tone** is everything. As an instructor, you must create an environment where a student can learn their best. Whether it is a private session or a group session (clinic), it all starts by learning everyone's **name**. To the individual being addressed, it is the sweetest word that they can hear. Because it is the sweetest of all words, a student's name must be **pronounced correctly**. Calling a student by their first name at least three times during a session is a must for a proper connection and it is the most important means of communication during a teaching session. Names have both significance and power. They define who we are. Correctly pronouncing someone's name means that you value and respect them and this alone will make a student's learning easier and more enjoyable. For a young student, it is the key to their existence and a means of recognition in society.

Next, a good instructor **may have** the proper objective, but a great instructor has a **plan** for their teaching sessions. It need not be a written plan, but it should be a plan of action that can be changed or amended depending on the situation. As your plan is being implemented, you must be aware of your student's reaction to what is being taught. You should ask yourself these questions. Are my students interested? Are they having success? Are they having fun? If the answer to any of these questions is no, then an adjustment in your plan needs to be made. This is where a great teacher becomes the artist. This creative part of tennis instruction is what separates the great teachers from the rest.

"Adjust to Change or Change to Dust." This quote was made germane by your author in a seminar given in 2004 and remains relevant today. If you want to avoid becoming a tennis teaching "dinosaur", you must stay abreast of changes in the tennis industry. An instructor may have been a great player in the days of **wooden racquets and gut strings,** but those days are gone. All teachers must be willing to change not only their lesson plans, but also their teaching philosophy in order to achieve desired outcomes. Teachers must keep this in mind when dealing with the variety of students that populate private and group settings. Students want to improve their tennis or they wouldn't be there. If you sense that your students are losing interest or not having fun, you must be willing to change in the moment. A new exercise or game might be just the remedy to facilitate a needed change. We know that **change** is the only constant in life, and the same is true in teaching tennis. If you want to stay relevant as a teacher, you must have an open mind in regard to changes in your teaching methods. Simple modifications can make a teacher great. **The teacher must be a lifelong learner** and great teachers are great learners. Changes that occur in the tennis teaching profession should be constantly monitored so that your teaching methods and philosophy are up to date. This is a compelling argument for joining a professional organization like the USPTA or the PTR. These organizations promote lifelong learning and are excellent resources for networking. You will gradually **become irrelevant** if you fail to stay abreast of your field.

[2] **USPTA Hall of Fame Coach Rick Macci** is a great example of a coach who has constantly evolved his teaching methods in order to stay abreast of the way tennis is currently played. Keep in mind that in the past Rick has coached tennis legends Serena and Venus Williams plus Grand Slam champions Andy Roddick and Maria Sharapova. In addition to his considerable coaching success, he currently spends 50 hours per week on court while continuing to develop players of all ages and abilities. Rick readily admits that today's professionals are both bigger and stronger than champions of the past and that changes in equipment, nutrition and recovery have combined to produce the most accomplished professional players in tennis history. Macci has incorporated these changes into his teaching philosophy and has recently focused on teaching the "ATP forehand"; a shot that Macci feels is now the dominant shot on the professional tour. He claims that everything in the tennis universe has changed and that "any parent, coach or teacher who isn't evolving every single day, they're really doing a disservice to the general public teaching the game of tennis." Rick also asserts that his tennis academy is among the world's finest and he promotes it with these words, "The Rick Macci Tennis Academy is pretty much the crown jewel of Palm Beach County…the place looks like Disneyland and Candyland. It's amazing. We have prize money tournaments, there are many pros, people can rent a court for $5…the place is rocking and rolling every day." Rick sums up his teaching philosophy in these five words: "Love, passion, consistency, dedication and persistence." Despite his heavy work schedule, the 66 year-old still exudes the passion and energy needed to deliver his teaching philosophy to his students, parents and coaches.

Good and Bad changes: We all know that the world is changing; sometimes in ways that are beneficial for everyone and sometimes in ways that are dreadful. The same can be said for modifications made by an instructor in the pursuit for tennis improvement. In the view of the instructor, the adjustment may have succeeded in the desired outcome. The teacher is satisfied that a positive change has been made and a period of improvement will surely follow. The student however, may have a different view. The student may realize that a change in their technique has been made and may trust the instructor's vision that an improved outcome will certainly follow. However, in the mind of the student, the end result might be quite different. Only after a year, five years or longer, will a student be able to discern if real improvement has made and whether the adjustment has been valuable. The **long and short-term view both count** and must be considered by every outstanding teacher.

You must be **invested** in a student's outcome. Outcomes of all teaching sessions should be of primary interest. A great teacher should not only teach in the moment, but have a considerable interest in the **results.** You should want your student to come back on a regular basis and ultimately to enjoy tennis for a lifetime. Too often instructors might teach in the moment, but concern themselves with the amount of money they are making now or later. If this is your motivation, you will be a colossal failure as an instructor and will never make it as a top teacher. The instruction that students receive should be top-notch, whether you are making $5.00 per hour or $500 per hour. Once your lesson fee has been established, money should not be a primary objective when teaching. If making money is your main objective, there are many other ways to make money as a tennis professional. For example, if you happen to be a Tennis Director at a country club or municipal facility, equipment sales, stringing, tennis balls, league fees and the organizing of tournaments are all possible avenues of revenue. There are very few tennis professionals that become wealthy by teaching only. **Multiple avenues of revenue** are the key for achieving financial security as a tennis professional.

Parental Coaching: Teaching your own child can be fraught with pitfalls. However, there are some examples of high profile players and their parents that have succeeded in reaching the highest level of professional tennis. Richard Williams and his two daughters Venus and Serena have risen from humble beginnings to reach the top of the professional tennis world. Andy Murray and his tennis-teaching mother Judy have reached the summit of men's tennis. Sophia Kenin, under the guidance of her father Alex, won the 2020 Australian Open. But a word of caution should be noted about these successful player-parent combinations. For every success story, there are thousands of player-parent combinations that have **destroyed families**. The ongoing conflict of the teacher's role and the role of the parent can be exhausting and negative results can be truly devastating for all involved. A tennis parent/teacher must be a **parent first.** If not, problems will surely follow. Most successful relationships between player and parent have occurred in families who come from impoverished backgrounds or from a parent who is a professional tennis teacher. The lesson here is that the pathway to professional tennis success is long and arduous. Consistent parental support is the best way to keep families together. Parents must both be able to encourage their children and ultimately **accept reality** when expectations and goals are not met.

Positive directives only are highly recommended: When teaching use only positive statements to covey what you want. Telling students **what not to do** will be counterproductive. Don't hit it that way; you have the wrong grip; don't do it that way; are all negative directives that will confuse a student's subconscious mind. Clear, concise instruction like; try this grip; swing this way; try this; are all positive directives that will yield better results and make you an exceptional teacher. Your students will better understand you and retain the guidance you provide.

Consistency is a valuable key to becoming a better teacher. Here we are not talking about the consistency of your forehand or serve or even your teaching methods. By consistency, we mean things like showing up for your class on time; being prepared for peak performance on a daily basis; dressing like you mean it and ending every class on time. Every one's **time is valuable** and your students are no different. You must consistently set the standard for a timely session. By being consistent in everything you do, your students will do the same.

Promotion: To be a successful teacher, you must be a promoter. You should promote **yourself, your students and your programs**. You can promote yourself through seminars, websites, blogs and articles written in prominent tennis magazines. The best way to advocate for yourself is by volunteering to give seminars at a USPTA or PTR national convention. You might consider heading a divisional workshop. You may also contribute articles to USPTA's *Addvantage* Magazine. A good way to promote your students is to network with sport reporters and editors of your local newspaper. You then must keep them updated with the progress of your best students. Your programs can be publicized through your club or facility website. Postings in the pro shop or activity area will keep your members updated on all lesson programs, leagues, tournaments and mixers.

Technique: Individuals, **yes; robots, no.** Great instructors need to have the teaching flexibility to allow every student to develop their own individual style. Many instructors try to force students to adopt a style (technique) of what **they think** is the best and most efficient way to play tennis. This "one size fits all" approach is seldom successful in allowing students to reach their full potential. There are only **two** requirements for playing excellent tennis. They are: **hitting the ball over the net inside the lines** and **covering the court**. How an individual does those two things depends on their talent and athleticism. Superb athletes who have great hand-eye coordination can become great players if they have had years of practice and sufficient exposure to other great players. This exposure can be acquired through practice or in tournaments, but tournament play is **the best exposure for a gifted athlete.** A great instructor must use caution when trying to make technique changes to any advanced player. The majority of the time the results are **tenuous**. There is a difference between **looking good** and being a **good match player**. Highly structured coaches can sometimes produce players that hit perfectly when given nice feeds, but tennis is a game of adjustments. **Nice feeds** are not seen in match play. The variety of shots that are encountered during a tennis contest are infinite and looking good will not win you matches. A great player must be able to improvise. Therefore, if your goal is to produce robotic players that look alike, strictly focusing on technique might achieve that goal; but if developing a good match player is your goal, then focusing on **practice** is a must. Tony Robbins, the #1 best-selling author, philanthropist and public speaker, said it best. **"Repetition is the mother of skill."** The skills required to be a great match player must be honed from years and years of practice. Some instructors will often give technique advice when addressing errors during match play. Bend your knees, watch the ball, and toss the ball higher can in general be good advice, but they seldom are the corrections needed to reduce **specific** errors. Errors will generally have corrections that are unique to the individual error. In addition, a great teacher should include a significant amount of **targeted practice** (e.g., finishing points) in every lesson.

The Modern Backhand: Since the first Wimbledon Championships of 1877, the one handed backhand has been used by the overwhelming majority of professional and amateur players. This all changed in 1974 when Americans Chris Evert and Jimmy Connors won the Wimbledon Women's and Men's singles with two-handed backhands. [3] The 2020 WTA (Women's Tennis Association) rankings consist of 2 one-handed backhand players and 98 two-handed players. [4] The 2019 ATP rankings (Association of Tennis Professionals) has 15 one-handed players and 85 two-handed players. Putting those numbers together, means that 183 of the top 200 professionals play with **two-handed backhands**.

It is the **author's opinion**, that in the **modern er**a, the majority of players, at all levels will be able to hit **both** the two-handed and the one-handed backhand with equal skill and comfort. The one-handed shot will be most effective when hitting slice, drop shots and low volleys. The two-hander offers more power, disguise, more effective swing volleys and the ability to adjust to the high bouncing ball. This **transition** to the modern backhand will be facilitated by excellent teaching professionals who will teach young players and adults both the one-handed and two-handed backhands while explaining the advantages and disadvantages of both.

The Future's Elite Player: The elite professional players of the **distant future** will be able to play with two forehands and no backhand. These special players will start young (6 and under) and hit equally well off both sides, using a left-handed forehand and a right-handed forehand. In addition, they will serve right-handed in the deuce court and left-handed in the ad court. Even though they might be vulnerable to balls hit right at them, adjustments will be made to accommodate this shot with a one-handed backhand. [5] A preview of this type of player has recently made its debut in 2021 edition of the prestigious USTA Junior Orange Bowl International

Tennis Championship held on the clay courts of Salvador Park in Coral Gables, FL. After defeating Tam Sin Shang of Hong Kong and advancing to the quarterfinals, 11 year-old, 4-foot-6 tennis phenom Teodor Davidov had this to say about his ambidextrous style. "I love it and will always do it. I like to show them different spins." This two-handed forehand approach is the creation of his father Kalin, who has a master's degree in high sports performance and a bachelor's degree in physical education and tennis coaching. Teodor's father never intended for this two forehand approach to tennis to get his child a tactical advantage, but only wanted a balanced life for his son. Kalin puts it this way. "Yoga is a driving force in our family life, so I'm trying to use tennis as a method of self-development. I'm not just training a great tennis player, for me this is secondary. A balance life is our goal. Teodor follows a vegetarian, gluten-free diet, while eating right-handed. Many tennis observers have said that Teodor is fearless when he plays and goes all out on every shot regardless of the score. Currently there are two playing professionals that play with two forehands. Russia's Evgenia Kulikovskaya, who has been ranked in the world's top 100 and 966th ranked Korean Cheong-Eui Kim. Teodor says this of his own professional aspirations. "I don't have any expectations of myself as long as I give it my best."

Relationship between intent and form: Tennis is a sport of adjustments. A student may have perfect forehand when hitting on a ball machine, but the harsh reality is that no two balls that are hit in a tennis match are the same (similar maybe, but not the same). The variety of shots one is forced to play in a match situation require different techniques. In a single point, a player may be required to hit a serve, forehand, backhand, volley, overhead, lob and drop shot. These shots necessitate grip changes, different contact points, and various court positions that must occur constantly throughout a match. The **serve** is the only shot where

18

the player is in complete control. A great server must be able to replicate accurate tosses and swing paths while throwing the racquet head up and over the ball. Basketball foul shots and golf swings are other actions that require a duplication of movement where hitting a ball that is predictable. The use of **video** can be extremely helpful when striving for excellence as a golfer or tennis server. This ability to reproduce the same swing is demanded for anyone wishing to become a professional player. Great teachers must be able to create teaching sessions where adjustments to various shots and situations are required. Practice points are an integral part of any lesson and can be created by the instructor or an assistant. When swing modifications are called for, the teacher can isolate the required shot and recommend the appropriate response.

Tell Me Why: Let's look at some specific errors and then make some commonsense corrections. Hitting groundstrokes in the net is a common error made by amateur players that can be easily corrected by reminding students that clearing the net by **3 feet or more** is the objective and that **only** by consistently clearing the net can you learn to keep the ball in the court. When this error is made, well-meaning instructors will often tell students to **bend their knees** as if to imply that hitting into the net is a lack of knee bend. We have all seen even top professionals hitting into the net while squatting for a low ball. Instead, opening up the racquet and making sure of the proper net clearance makes more sense. Another common error is hitting serves in the net. A well-meaning coach might advise the student to **toss the ball higher**. The proper correction is to make sure you **hit up** on the ball and clear the net by at least two feet. Sometimes students will try to hit into the service box instead of clearing the net first. Since the server sees the service box by looking **through the net**, and since the line of sight goes through the net, a service fault in the net can be a common occurrence. The proper thought process when serving and under pressure is; **"over the net and in the box"**. Players should avoid **allowing** the **net** to judge their faults. Instead, let your opponent or some high-speed camera technology determine whether your serve is in or out. A **good error ratio for service faults** should be two long for every serve hit into the net.

Errors and More Errors: How should errors be corrected once they are made? The proper correction should be made **mentally and in the moment** immediately after the error is made. The following are examples of two errors made by two different **professionals** that should have been corrected in the moment. Both players were playing doubles, indoors with good lighting, no wind or sun and excellent backgrounds. In the first instance, the player, after letting a high lob bounce, and standing on the service line in the middle of the court, hit the overhead about a yard long in the direction of the ad court player. In the second instance, the player, after letting a high lob bounce, and standing a step behind the baseline in the middle of the court, hit the overhead in the middle of the net. Let's review the **mental** corrections that should have been made. When standing on the service line in the middle of the court, the proper **target** is the opposite service line. In the second instance, the correct **window** is 3 feet over the net. An excellent exercise for any player is to practice serving from various spots on the court and aiming for the correct target or window. Remember that you have the whole court available, not just the service boxes. Great margins are possible when having the right picture in your mind when striking the ball. When making any error while playing a point, one must make the mental correction and then proceed to play in the **present**. One should always have a short memory concerning previous scores and errors. If the proper corrections are unknown to the competing player, consulting with a great teaching professional is a must.

No one can know everything about anything for very long: A well-meaning instructor with many years of playing and teaching experience may teach their entire career using the same teaching philosophy. Great coaches must be life-long learners and be able and willing to **change** when appropriate.

Should You Have a High Toss or Low Toss? A knowledgeable teacher should be able to explain the advantages and disadvantages of a high and a low service toss. The high toss allows for more topspin when hitting a **kick** serve, but the toss is more difficult to control. Strong to moderate winds can also wreak havoc with the high toss. A lower toss makes it easier to hit a slice **serve** which will have a lower bounce and a greater sweeping action. The **Control** of the low toss is easier and wind issues are largely removed. So what is high and what is low? Low tosses (ball drop of 6 inches or less) should be high enough so that a full extension of the racquet at contact can be achieved. A high toss might be 6 feet or more above a player's full extension. The best ball toss height is a personal one and will probably involve some experimentation. In general, left-handers may prefer a lower toss in order to make the slice serve in the **ad court** more effective against right-handers. A right-handed server might prefer a higher toss if using the kick serve frequently. This is especially helpful in the ad court, where the kick serve **out wide** must cross the high part of the net. Whatever ball toss is chosen, the height should be the same for all serves, so that **disguise** can still be achieved.

No Such Thing as an Easy Shot: During match play, you will probably encounter "setups" or balls that should be put away. In matches that are not competitive or when playing a lesser opponent, this might be considered a routine shot; a shot that should be made every time. However, the difficulty of a "setup" is determined by a variety of things. Some of these are an opponent's position, your position, an opponent's speed, the closeness of the score, the pressure of the moment or an **unfriendly crowd**. If any or all of these factors are present, suddenly this "setup" is **no longer routine**. These so-called easy shots must be treated with the same focus and concentration that is given to each and every shot during a competitive match. They also need to be practiced. A former coach explained the shot to me this way. **"There's a reason why they are called easy shots. Because they are easy to miss."**

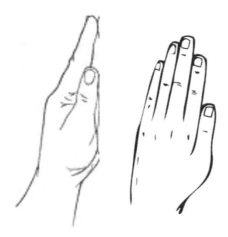

Left-handed Pronation

Pronation Demonstration Explanation: Accomplished coaches will clearly demonstrate wrist pronation when serving. This very important concept allows for maximum power and the proper grip (continental) when serving. Elite teachers should be able to first demonstrate with the hand; then with a choked racquet and finally with the hand on the grip. As the server is swinging up to the ball, the extension of the arm and the pronation of the wrist should occur simultaneously. A nice **loose wrist** and arm action should be emphasized. The idea is to **throw** the racquet at the ball, while holding on to the racquet. It may be helpful for beginning and intermediate servers to try and throw old racquets over the back fence. It is important to be sure no one is on the other side.

Equipment: A great instructor is well versed in the best racquets and stringing practices for all levels of players. [6] For advanced players like Roger Federer and Serena Williams, hybrid stringing is a must for peak performance and comfort. Roger and Serena both use a combination of natural gut and polyester, which are the strings of choice of many professional players. The classic hybrid string pattern uses polyester on the mains and natural gut on the crosses. The choice of Roger and Serena is the **inverse** hybrid string pattern which uses gut on the mains and polyester on the crosses. Roger strings his *Wilson Pro Staff RF 97 Autograph* mains with *Wilson Natural Gut* at 27 kgs (59.4 lbs.) and the crosses with *Luxilon ALU Rough* at 25.5 kgs (56.1 lbs.). Serena strings her 28" *Wilson Blade SW 102 Autograph* mains with *Wilson Natural Gut* at 29.5 kgs (65 lbs.) and the crosses with *Luxilon 4G* at 29 kgs (64 lbs.) Other top pros that use the inverse hybrid stringing are Kei Nishikori, Felix Auger-Aliassime and Jo-Wilfried Tsonga. Kei strings his racquets much looser than most top professionals; 39 pounds for the mains (Wilson natural gut) and 37 pounds for the crosses (Luxilon – Element). Since the majority of a racquet's playability comes from the mains, the reverse hybrid pattern may be an excellent choice for players seeking comfort and power from their strings. If a player is playing with both the mains and crosses with polyester and is having arm problems, a switch to a hybrid string pattern should take pressure off your arm and joints. The weight of your racquet is another thing to consider when finding the right balance between playability and comfort. Most top professional use a heavier racquet than those sold to the general public. There are many things players need to consider when choosing the proper stringing pattern. Some of these are: the **durability** of the string, the **playability** of the racquet, the string bed **stiffness**, the proper balance between **power and control**, **spin** potential, making the racquet **easier on the arm** and finally the **cost.**

Learn from Others: A great teacher can always learn from others. Often great insight can be obtained from other teachers, particularly instructors with extensive experience.

Limitations: Outstanding teachers are aware of their own limitations. Not every instructor is physically, mentally or knowledgeable enough to effectively teach every age and talent level. There are many potential students that are in want of instruction. Ages 4-6 require an instructor who is patient and great with young children. Advanced teenagers and adults need instructors who have the proper background and experience to coach exceptional talents. Knowing one's strengths and weaknesses will allow teachers and students alike to maximize their abilities.

Love: Most tennis teachers like tennis or they wouldn't be teaching. But the best tennis teachers not only like tennis, they **love it**. Everything about the sport consumes them and that often leaves time for little else. Just as the top professionals are consumed with practice, tournaments and travel, the great tennis teachers are absorbed in all aspects of teaching. Unfortunately this can result in neglect to family and friends. However, a great teacher **will balance** these commitments to assure a well-rounded life.

Discipline of scheduling: Many outstanding tennis teachers want to teach forever or when they can no longer perform. The best instructors recognize the importance of scheduling. Proper scheduling will enable them to teach for the long term. Some instructors many teach up to 60 hours per week because they are young and strong and the demand for their services are robust. Many instructors that overschedule end up teaching while injured and consequently develop life-long damage to their body that cannot be totally repaired.

The **conditioning** habits of the best teachers should not be overlooked. These teachers strive to take care of themselves so that they can perform at their peak every day. They tend to have **healthy diets** and exercise on a regular basis. A well-conditioned teacher, who sets a good example for their pupils, will win the respect and admiration of their students. This can lead to fruitful learning environment where students can learn their best.

A Connection: Great teachers are able to connect with students by using a combination of **humor and wit**. This connection can last long after the lesson is over and can be a powerful catalyst for the long-term enjoyment of playing tennis.

[7] **Who should Students practice with?** A knowledgeable instructor realizes that practice matches are a **crucial element** in achieving tennis improvement? But what kind of practice matches? Some players erroneously think that if they could play a match with Roger Federer once a week, that improvement would surely follow. **Nothing could be further from the truth**. Unless you are among the top 200 players in the world, you may improve your ball pick-up skills but nothing else. The only way **you might improve** is if Roger agrees to give you a weekly lesson. The best practice partners are those that are consistent and do a great job covering the court. In addition the majority of your practice matches should be with players you can beat so that you develop a **winning attitude** and convince your **subconscious mind** that you are a winner and can close out matches even if you are playing poorly.

Improvement and Enjoyment should be the steadfast goal of all great instructors: For most, improvement is not easily achieved and will take time and effort. For a tennis player to progress, it will take lots of practice and the right kind of practice. **So what is the right kind of practice?** Many players and some teachers mistakenly believe that spending hour upon hour rallying from the backcourt is the best and fastest way to improve. Although some progress can be made with consistent rally practice, the **best way** and the **fastest way** to improve is by practicing the shots that begin points (serve and service return) and the shots that finish points with **high margins** (volleys and overheads). The **experienced instructor** knows that young players can improve weekly, but the older, more experienced players are likely to **improve slowly**. Students **want**

to improve their tennis skills and many depend on their teaching professional to guide them in the proper direction. The sport of tennis, although constantly evolving, has an obligation to both players and fans to also improve. In fact all aspects of the tennis industry want and need improvement. This **desire to improve** is the essence of the human condition and a rare constant in an ever-changing world.

How can I hit fewer double faults? Well-meaning instructors will often spend time trying to improve a player's second serve in order to lessen double faults. Although this can be of some help, a better solution is to **improve the first serve**, so that fewer second serves have to be attempted. This will automatically reduce double faults. A good practice exercise is to drape a sheet over the net, so that the service box cannot be seen by the server. Then have someone on the other side, judge the serves to let the server know which are in and by how far.

Chapter 2
The Role of the Conscious and Subconscious Minds

A great teaching professional should have a clear understanding of the roles played by the conscious and subconscious minds. Communication of this role to students, particularly talented juniors is crucial for their proper mental and emotional development.

The Role of the Conscious Mind: During a competitive tennis match, the conscious mind should be focused on just two things; first, deciding what **shot to play next** and, if an error is made, mentally make the **proper correction**. If this pattern is consistently followed, a player's best tennis will most often be the result.

The Role of the Subconscious Mind: The subconscious mind wants to work in concert with the conscious mind and will do the very best it can to play great tennis at the conscious mind's direction. The conscious mind should focus on **what to do**, **not how** to do it. The subconscious mind, if programmed through hours and hours of practice, knows how to play tennis; it needs only **direction** from the conscious mind.

Errant ball tosses and double faults: Players who are prone to double fault under pressure can be greatly helped by an excellent professional. The ball toss is often targeted as the proper correction when dealing with faults. Often a well-meaning pro will instruct a student to redo a toss that is not in the "right place" or not perfect. This emphasis on ball toss can create **doubt** in a server's mind. The ball toss is part of the service motion and has been imprinted into the **subconscious mind** of each student, based on their play and practice habits. Judging each toss requires the **intervention of the conscious mind.** The only role the conscious mind should have when serving is to determine what serve to hit and where. After that determination is made, the subconscious mind should take over and hit the serve the conscious mind wants. All **negative** thoughts of the conscious mind must **be eliminated** before and during the service process.

What is the role of the conscious and subconscious mind when serving? Great instructors recognize the importance of the subconscious mind and how it relates to the conscious mind when playing a competitive tennis match. The subconscious mind is your computer and has made a record of everything that has happened in your life to date. It has also recorded your fears, likes, dislikes, goals, dreams and every thought that you have ever had. The subconscious mind is **non-judgmental**. It will only tell your conscious mind in an impartial and unfiltered way what it has recorded. Your conscious mind works in the present and can only look into a somewhat biased version of the future. You might think that your conscious mind can control you subconscious, but in fact the opposite is true. Every time your conscious mind wants to do something, it will check with your subconscious to see if it is permitted. For example, if for fun you decide on a dare to jump from the top of a twenty story building, your conscious mind will ask your subconscious if it is okay to jump. Your subconscious might say something like this, "No, don't jump; it will probably **kill you.**" Pressure packed tennis matches can create similar interactions between your conscious and subconscious mind. By way of illustration, if you happen to find yourself in the Wimbledon Singles Final against the all-time great Roger Federer and you are serving and have reached match point for you, your nerves will surely be tested in this pressure-packed setting. At this moment, your conscious mind will ask your subconscious if it is okay to go ahead and win. Your subconscious mine, which will only tell you the truth will likely say this, "Roger is ranked number one in the world and you are number 216 and you've never beaten him before." At this moment, your pulse, blood pressure and breathing rate start to increase and your conscious mind, since it is receiving no encouragement from the subconscious decides to take over. The result; fault; double fault; you lose and your blood pressure and heart rate quickly return to normal. The problem is that your conscious mind does not know how to hit a 130 mph serve with topspin to the backhand. Your conscious mind only did this the very **first time**. However, your subconscious mind which has been conditioned through years and years of **practice** can do this consistently. So then, how do we engage our subconscious mind at this pivotal moment of the match? The key is visualization the night before and creating that future you've always dreamed. Before playing Roger, you make your dream come true. You prepare for this occasion by visualizing this moment; playing points with no errors, the crowd noise, hitting the winning shot, shaking Roger's hand, receiving the 5 million dollar check, and speaking to the media afterwards. You do this with total focus, removing all negative thoughts. The next day when that moment arrives, and when your conscious mind asks your subconscious if it's okay to win, your subconscious which cannot differentiate between fantasy and reality, will tell you the truth. **"You beat him last night."**

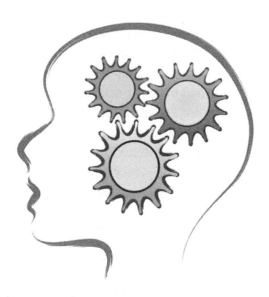

Positive directives and the subconscious mind: Assume you are playing tennis and would like to hit a slice serve on the line. Your subconscious can and will deliver if you have practiced sufficiently. All you have to think is "hit a slice serve on the line." However, in a tight situation, **if** you are thinking **"don't double fault"**; the subconscious mind will not understand what you want. If you don't want to double fault, then what do you want? A soft serve to the middle of the court? The subconscious only understands positive directives. Let's consider another example. Assume that you are a Major League pitcher who is pitching in the 7th game of a World

Series. It is the ninth inning and you are one out away from victory. Your team is ahead by one run, there is a runner on third, two outs and the count is 3 balls and 2 strikes. The hitter at the plate is a notorious home run hitter who loves the low inside pitch. Your catcher and your manager converge on the mound and both give you the same message. "This guy is a great inside low ball hitter. Whatever you do, **don't** throw it low inside." After you tell them that you understand, your mind keeps repeating this negative directive and your subconscious hears you but does not comprehend the objective. Here comes the pitch; **low inside**, the hitter yanks it out of the ball park for a home run. They win and your team loses. So what is the best advice your catcher and manager could give you in this pressure-packed situation? How about "Throw it high outside." Your subconscious will understand this straight-forward positive directive and likely deliver. Remember, the worst thing to do when you are nervous and in a tight situation is to think a negative directive, e.g. "don't double fault". If doubts creep into your thoughts when you're on the big stage and feeling the pressure, tell yourself, **"Que Sera Sera (Whatever Will Be Will Be)"**. Remember that your conscious mind **cannot see or change the future**. Then focus on a positive outcome and **let your subconscious** make it happen.

Breathing Techniques: If you have ever watched a basketball game, you may have noticed that the **good** foul shooters take a long, deep breath before shooting. When watching a baseball game, you may have noticed the hitters doing the same thing. What does this have to do with the conscious and subconscious mind? The answer is that this breathing technique clears the pathway between the conscious and subconscious so that the subconscious can follow the direction of the conscious mind. Tennis is no different. Great servers, particularly in crucial moments will take one or two deep breaths before serving. This will allow the subconscious mind to operate at peak efficiency and make it easier to follow the direction of the conscious mind. Years and years of practice have programmed the subconscious mind to duplicate serves that are needed in the moment. Many professional players will often **grunt** when striking the ball. This sudden exhale of air will then be followed by a deep inhale and over the course of a match will allow a player to compete in a relaxed state.

Chapter 3
Ages 4-6 – Fun First

ages **4-6: Fun must be first.** When teaching this impressionable age group, patience will be necessary to accomplish the goal of having your young students enjoy their session and have fun. A variety of activities will stimulate these young minds and keep them coming back for more. These activities should include games and ball judgment skills that will complement their skill with the racquet as they learn. Ball skills might include dropping the tennis ball and trying to catch it; first with two hands and then with one (alternate with each hand); tossing the ball in the air and then catching with two hands and then with one. Instruction can then proceed to playing catch with a classmate or instructor. Bouncing the ball during these toss and catch activities will help with the judgment of pressurized balls later on. Racquet skills should start with balancing the ball on the face of the racquet (student may use two hands). Bouncing the ball on the ground with the racquet and then in the air are nice progressions for this age group. If a student or class cannot accomplish particular exercises, focus on what they can do and not what they can't.

No one gets hurt: Instructors should keep this approach in the forefront of all activities. Fun cannot and will not be had if someone gets hurt. Since most activities and games involve ball skills, it is a good idea to keep racquets on the ground unless the use of a racquet is involved in a specific activity. When using racquets for a particular exercise, be sure to have proper spacing so that no one gets hit with a racquet.

Talking with parents: Communication with the child's parents after each session is extremely important in order to maintain a positive viewpoint of lessons learned. Anything positive a child does during your teaching sessions should be relayed to a parent. It is then likely that these positive observations will be repeated at home. This reinforcement of the child's progress should encourage these young children and hopefully they will identify their achievements with tennis.

Private or Semi-private lessons: When working with 4-6 year olds, 30 minute sessions are recommended. Children of this age have short attention spans and sessions lasting more than 30 minutes are generally counterproductive. Ball drills that involve tossing and catching are excellent places to start. The toss should be underhand and bounce to the student. Catches can be made with both hands. This drill will help hand eye coordination and will allow the young student to judge the bounce. All exercises that develop the aforementioned skills will be helpful once the racquet is introduced. Balancing the ball on the racquet is an excellent exercise and students may use both hands. Placing the ball on the racquet's face and running under control from baseline to net and back in a good next step. Practice swings on both forehand and backhand can be done with instructor demonstrating with student. Emphasis should be placed on the **follow-through**. Finishing every lesson with dropping and hitting the ball makes for a nice ending. Initially instructor should be the ball dropper. Once the student is making ball contact the student can then do the ball dropping.

Group Lessons: Various games are a principal component in teaching young children, particularly in group lessons. These group lessons (clinics) should last no more than 1 hour and include one or two water breaks. All of the previous exercises mentioned in the private and semi-private section should be included here. Often grade school physical education instructors that play tennis at the club level will make the best instructors. They are used to organizing large groups and can relate to children of this age. Most everyone likes games, especially children ages 4-6 and assorted relays should be at the top of the list. These relays will keep the child active and interested in what is being taught. An instructor's imagination is the best source of ideas that will both challenge and entertain each child. As long as each activity involves either the ball or ball and racquet, this type of training will guide each child toward improving their tennis skills.

Tennis Camps for ages 4-6: These camps tend to be popular with parents, because they might last 3-4 hours and give parents some free time. Often these camps operate like day care centers to babysit children while parents get a needed break. In my opinion, when it comes to a child's long term interest in tennis, these types of camps can do more harm than good. Children at this age need constant stimulation and a 3-4 hour teaching session is a tough assignment for the best of teachers. Sometimes these sessions are offered because they can be a great source of income, but not a great source for learning. Other factors for parents to consider are the location of the clinic. Is it indoors or outdoors? Clinics offered in warm-weather climates can sometimes be quite hot and sunny. Parents should be aware of the possibility of sunburn and overheating when deciding on this type of instruction. A child's long-term interest in tennis should be of primary importance when deciding on the proper instructional format.

Popcorn tennis is a fun activity especially designed for 4-6 year olds. I will use as an example a group lesson with 4 students. The instructor places four balls on his racquet, and with his free hand on the balls, moves his racquet in a circular motion while saying, "The popcorn is popping," Or something similar. The instructor then throws the balls up in the air with his racquet. Each student is then asked to place one ball on the instructor's racquet, as the instructor places four additional balls on his racquet. With eight tennis balls the popcorn tossing is repeated. The students are then asked to bring the instructor two balls; the instructor adds eight and the tossing continues. The photo below shows 12 balls in the air.

Photo: "popcorn" at Huffhines Tennis Center Dallas, TX 2020

Frustration should be avoided and lessons of all types should be fast-paced. When an exercise is too difficult for these toddlers, an outstanding instructor will notice. Too much time spent on one activity can lead to boredom. There are many activities that involve footwork and arm movements that can replicate movements in tennis. These can be done without racquets   Side to side footwork, ready positions and reaching "tall for the ball" are all stimulating and fun. These drills can all be done without racquets. All that is required is a creative imagination from the instructor. Balloons, bean bags, and tennis balls are some of the many accessories that can aid the innovative teacher to eventually link the tennis ball with the racquet.

When combining **racquets** and balls, a proper racquet will make exercises easier and more enjoyable for all. Some youngsters may have a parent's racquet that is too long or too heavy. For these situations, used inexpensive junior racquets should be available. This can sometimes lead to a sale that will make a great starter racquet. The parent has then made an additional investment in the child's **tennis future**.

Chapter 4
Ages 7-10 – Ball and Racquet Skills

*A*ges 7-10: For this age group, the **racquet** should be a part of each exercise. These children should be able to integrate the racquet with the ball. Recommended length of private and semi-private lessons should be ½ hour for beginners and 1 hour for advanced players. Each session should include 10 minutes of **serving**. Everything that was said in chapter 2 should be part of the lesson structure for this age group. Fun, communicating with parents and injury free lessons will still be important. Since this age group will be swinging racquets, especially in clinic settings, proper student spacing will need the instructor's full attention. Beginners should work toward dropping and hitting with a nice finish.

Instructor feeds should be part of each session. Advanced players should be attempting controlled rallies with the teacher. Additional skill challenges should include, rolling the ball around the edge of the racquet frame; bouncing the ball on the ground with the racquet; bouncing the ball up in the air with one side of the racquet face; alternating sides of the racquet face while bouncing the ball up in the air.

Group Lessons (one hour is ideal): This is the perfect time to introduce students to the ball machine. One ball machine and two instructors for teaching **eight students** is best. While four students are hitting forehands and backhands on the ball machine, the other students are practicing serving on an adjacent court. When not hitting on the ball machine, advanced players can practice serving and rallying on the adjacent court. Ideally the ball machine is set up in the middle of the court on the service line. The ball machine is then programmed to alternate soft feeds to the deuce and ad courts. Advanced players can hit one at a time alternating forehand and backhands until missing. The time between feeds should be just challenging enough to push students to recover quickly between shots. Beginning players should form two lines (two players each line) and do stationary hitting (4 shots each) one at a time. Beginning players would hit 4 forehands and switch to the backhand line and repeat. The remaining two players would hit 4 backhands and switch lines; in order to avoid injury, instructors should make sure they have proper spacing.

Clinics: (1 ½ hours - 16 students or more). Organization is key for this type of instruction. Large numbers of students can pose uncommon problems for lesson planning. A great way to begin each session in to incorporate a liberal number of practice swings for each named stroke (Make sure you have proper spacing). On one court, students can imitate an instructor in front of the class, while the rest of the instructors in back can help students individually. Once practice swings have concluded, a **maximum** of 4 students per court is ideal to continue student advancement. Segregating students according to age and/or ability should help different exercises run smoothly.

The Advanced, Gifted, and Athletic Child: These children will gain maximum improvement in 1 hour private lessons per week with an accomplished teacher who has been a player at the college level. These gifted players should be given practice on all shots with a particular emphasis on the serve. A portion of the lesson should consist of practice points with the student. The teacher should play at a pace comfortable for the student, while hustling and playing no-miss tennis. These points should make up roughly

¼ of the lesson. Once a student has made an error, the shot should be replayed and the point should continue. Teachers should make sure the student is hitting the same shot, to the appropriate area of the court when correcting the error. All points are replayed just once. Service return errors and double faults should be replayed. Always finish the lesson with some **student successes**. The student should feel special after the lesson and believe that progress was made. If possible, this progress should be reinforced with the parent afterwards and successes highlighted. The teacher should emphasize the importance of practicing between lessons. Always remember that the long-term interest of the student and parent are the teacher's greatest gift when delivering exceptional instruction.

Chapter 5

Ages 11-18 – Social and Gifted Teen

ges 11-18: Preteens and Teenagers can be divided into three broad categories. Beginners, intermediates and advanced players should be coached using different formats. Beginners will do better in group or clinic settings. Intermediates in semi-private or private settings and advanced players will thrive best in private lessons. Divisions are decided partly on talent and skill level and partly on aspirations. Some advanced players may aspire to play college tennis or become a professional player. Intermediates may want to play on their high school or junior high team. Beginners may only want to be able to play socially or with their friends. Keep in mind that children can develop rapidly at this age and their dreams and aspirations may change as their skills improve.

Advanced teens are best served in one hour lessons once per week. The recommendations given for teaching these players are similar to the advice given in chapter 2, except the coaching should be done by a certified former college or professional player. There should be a focus on serve and service return. Practice points should be played with the instructor who will play consistent tennis, playing at a comfortable pace for the student. Errors need to be replayed with an emphasis on finishing points with good margin. Points that end up with the student on the defensive should be finished by the instructor and a new point started. Preteens should begin all points as the server. Teens should be given equal practice on serve and service returns. An attempt should be made to provide instruction and practice on these four areas; serve, overheads, service returns and practice points. Taking into consideration a student's individual needs, an appropriate amount of time should be allotted to address specific areas. Practice between lessons **should be emphasized**. Students should not be frustrated after the completion of their lesson, but should be pleased with their progress.

Academy vs. Private Instruction: Tennis academies can provide valuable instruction for extremely gifted teens, but there are some **drawbacks**. The primary benefit obtained by talented juniors is mostly gained through practicing with their peers. These associations with other talented juniors from different parts of the world offer benefits that cannot be obtained from local clubs or municipal facilities. It has been my experience in working with many talented juniors that this benefit is limited for the following reasons. Teen-age boys and girls can be easily enticed by the adventures offered by their larger world. Teens away from home are often tempted to engage in partying, drinking, not studying and a myriad of activities that will stall their long-term improvement. Counselors that could caution teens of these temptations are seldom available. Although some academies employ knowledgeable and experienced pros, a teen's exposure to these professionals is often limited. Bad habits of frustration, temper tantrums and cheating learned from practice partners can easily become part of a teen's psychological makeup. In addition, the cost of attending these academies is expensive and not affordable for many families.

The **advantages** of a teen staying home and developing are **many** and I will list a few. A certified former college/professional player will be invested and interested in the teen's development both as a tennis player and a person. There will be no one, with the exception of the teen's immediate family that will **take more interest** in this player than the **local pro**. Instructions and tournament schedules can be tailored to fit a teen's aspirations and needs. A great professional is expected to exhibit **impeccable behavior** on the court even when challenged by a gifted teen's play during practice points or matches. This faultless behavior will usually be imitated by the teen over time. It should be emphasized that **emotions can and must be controlled**. A great pro will teach this gifted teen not only everything he or she knows, but will give the teen a practice schedule designed to eventually beat the teacher. Being with your friends is important for a developing teen as are the myriad of activities made available at school. Most parents will encourage their children to excel in their studies while they are excelling on the court. A teen's success can be publicized in the local media which may help their preparation for future accomplishments. A knowledgeable pro will also recognize any limitations a player might have and keep expectations reasonable for the player and parent. All of this plus **cost** should be considered when deciding a course of action.

Grips: Most **talented** juniors who have started tennis early (4-8 years old) have developed their own style by the time they are a teenager. Specifically, **grips** have been adopted that are appropriate for a teen's timing and physical makeup. This is especially true for talented teens who have had success in junior tournaments. Any new instructors should take **great care** when considering grip changes or going from a two-handed backhand to a one-hander (e.g. Pete Sampras). This can often happen when a talented teen changes instructors. Changes for this teen should be of the type that correct errors and offer benefits almost immediately.

Angle up on Service Return: As teens develop, facing bigger serves will become the norm instead of the unusual. A server may use the common tactic of serving wide in both the ad and deuce courts followed with an aggressive shot to the open court. In order to combat this common plan of attack, the server must **angle up** in both the ad and deuce courts. Angling up means to move at **right angles** to the direction of the incoming serve. Many players will incorrectly move **parallel** to the baseline to return these wide serves and will give up valuable court position. As a consequence, this makes the covering of the open court problematic.

The Squat: When viewing a professional match on television you might occasionally see a player squat while swinging in an attempt to play a groundstroke when hitting a low ball. This **poor technique** generally stems from well-meaning instructors who are trying to help teens avoid hitting the net at all costs when dealing with low balls in the backcourt. However, the purpose of the knee bend is to enable a player to gain added lift when hitting a groundstroke. This additional lift enables a player to add both power, spin and surety of shot, particularly in crucial situations. On the other hand, bending the knees is a must for the **low volley**. Squatting while swinging during a groundstroke is not only very difficult to do, but is **of little help** in clearing the net. Obvious things like opening the racquet face slightly, dropping the racquet head or aiming higher are much better solutions and easier to do.

Private Instruction for the Gifted Teen: In addition to giving a talented teenager a 1 hour lesson per week, an exceptional professional will map out the pupil's practice and match schedule. Proper practice with a ball machine should be part of a student's weekly routine. (A detailed practice schedule for the serve is given in chapter 5, pages 41-45, *A Modern Guide for Tennis Improvement* [8], by J. R. Williams). Since the serve is the most **important shot** in tennis, I have reprinted the proper service practice for **real improvement** here.

The Serve and Hitting Winners – Advancing to 5.0

Every good player at the 5.0 level owns their **serve**. Since serving is the single **most important shot** in tennis and the key to your confidence in tight matches, this is a good place to start. While being 6' 5" or taller can make it easier to generate power and to achieve margin, it is **not** the key ingredient to having a **great** serve. In order to have a great serve, you must be able to hit your spots on all serves at any time, particularly in tight situations. This requires **lots** of **practice**.

To gain **real improvement** in your serve, you will need to hit 100 serves a day, 6 days a week for two months. After that time real improvement will be noticed by you and anyone you play. How you practice is crucial for this improvement to take place. Your first 50 serves should be ½ to ¾ speed and hit for placement in this order. For right handers in the deuce court, make 2 in a row down the tee (hit flat), and two in a row out wide (slice); then 2 in a row down the middle. Repeat in the ad court. The next 50 should be at full speed (hard as you can) repeating the placement with focus on a quality slice out wide in the deuce court if you are right handed; the ad court if you are left handed. In summary, for all 100 serves, you will hit all six spots, moving to the next spot only after you have made two in a row. If you are left-handed, start in the ad court with the slice out wide. During the second month, you continue to do the same thing with this exception, three in a row should be made before moving to the next spot. After two months, in order to maintain this service improvement, you should continue to practice the same routine 3 times a week. An emphasis should be put on **consistently clearing the net**, since you are trying to take the net out of play. Placing targets in the service corners will help your depth and net clearance. There are some who might think faster improvement can be made by hitting more serves. This is not the case. More than 100 serves will risk arm injury, so patience is the key.

Refer to **Fig 1** for proper practice.

Right Handers – Deuce Court: A (slice), B (flat, slice or topspin), C (flat)

Left Handers – Deuce Court: A (topspin), B (flat, slice or topspin), C (slice)

Right Handers – Ad Court: A (slice), B (flat, slice or topspin), C (topspin)

Left Handers – Ad Court: A (flat), B (flat, slice or topspin), C (slice)

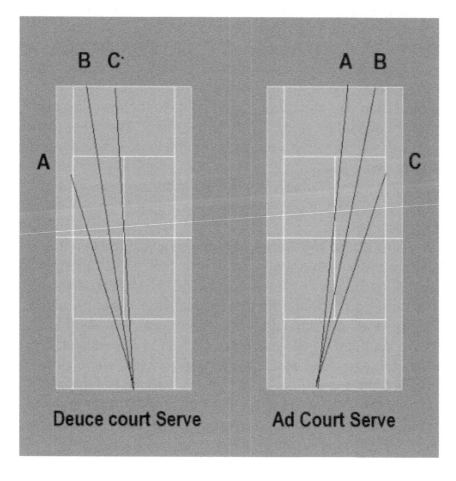

Fig 1

Proper service technique – Since at least 80% of your power on the serve comes from the **wrist**, the proper grip is crucial for maximizing power and putting your wrist in the proper position at impact. The grip should be a "continental grip" with your wrist aligned with the racquet's edge. You should attempt to **throw the racquet head up and over the ball** with a loose wrist while still holding on to the racquet. A good exercise to gain the proper feel is to try and throw old racquets up and over the back fence (make sure no one is in the area). The ball toss height should be approximately 3 inches above the intended point of contact at full stretch. Some instructors recommend higher tosses, but this makes serving in the wind and serving with sun in your eyes much more difficult. There is little or no advantage to tossing the ball a foot or more higher than you can reach. Being able to replicate the toss and the point of contact is the key to consistency. Twenty percent of your power will come by properly using the legs. When the ball toss is at its peak, your legs should be bent and ready to push upward as you swing. Finally, you should establish a consistent rhythm by synchronizing your toss with your racquet preparation.

Special Notes about the Serve: When discussing the serve with developing servers at this level, I try to emphasize the importance of the first serve. One of my favorite sayings is, "Missing a second serve will **cost you a point**, but the cumulative effect of missing your first serve will probably **cost you the match**." Remember that if you make your first serve, you will not have to hit a second. Another saying I am fond of is, "If you miss your first serve close, hit it again. If you miss your first serve badly or into the net, hit a different serve for your second." In addition, missing your first serve three times in a row is a danger signal, particularly if the serves are in the net. This is also a likely sign that you are nervous or tight. You should now slow down, take a few **deep breaths** and refocus. Finding your rhythm or "grove" is everything when serving and should be your **primary objective**. A serve that hits the tape or is a let has not been missed by inches but has been missed by feet. A one to two foot net clearance for advanced players should be your goal, not one or two inches. **The pressure of an important match can cause even the best servers at all levels to doubt themselves when serving in the big moments.**

A great example of this occurred in the Women's 2020 Australian Open Final featuring American Sofia Kenin and Venezuelan Garbine Muguruza. Garbine, who is a two-time Grand Slam champion, under normal circumstances is an excellent server. However, while serving at 2-5 in the third set, she hit 3 double faults including a double fault on match point to give the championship to Sofia. On the other hand, Kenin who made a lot of first serves, did not miss a second serve in 3 closely contested sets. The lesson to remember is, more often than not, the **serve** is the **deciding factor** in close pressure-packed matches.

[9,10] **Another great example** of major serving problems involving a **professional** player has surfaced in the results of world #2 Aryna Sabalenka. In the two tournaments leading up to the 2022 Australian Open, the Belarusian has averaged more than a double fault per service game in her last two losing matches. In her last four matches, she has served **60 double faults in 52 service games** (all in losing efforts). It has gotten so bad that she was reduced to serving underhand in portions of those matches. Who knows how bad it could have gotten without a temporary reprieve of serving a few points underhand. In her last losing effort to #93 ranked Swedish player Rebecca Peterson, things got so bad, that the umpire asked Aryna if **she was hurt**. Aryna replied, "No I'm not hurt, it's just **technical**." In her next service game, she broke down in tears.

The fix: The question then becomes; what should an outstanding instructor do now to help Aryna move forward and **fix her serve**? The author is sure that there are some teaching professionals that would recommend a **technique fix** for the world's #2. Others might recommend a **sport's psychologist**. Keep in mind that Aryna has hit thousands and thousands of serves in her lifetime and that Aryna has a **high** toss (approximately 6 to 8 feet above her outstretched hand) and there was a slight wind blowing those days (10 to 20 mph). Without knowing the history between Aryna and her current coach, I will make some educated guesses as to some possible fixes. My **best guess** is that her current coach has been working with her serve and is probably trying to make **some adjustments**. We all know that a high ball toss is more difficult to control than a lower one, particularly in the wind. (Nadal lets the ball drop about 2 inches before hitting). Aryna lets the ball drop approximately 3 feet before hitting. We would next need to know how long Aryna has had the high ball toss. If it has been a fairly **recent development**, a **lower toss** might do the trick. If she has had a **high** toss since her **junior days** (which would be **unusual**), then a lower toss would **probably not work**. Since she has hit thousands and thousands of serves a certain way, a technique change is probably **not the solution**. One other thought worth a try is covering the net with a sheet. The **sheet** is placed over the net so that the server **cannot see** the service boxes; then **clearing the net** consistently can be easily done. A camera can be used to identify the ball placement on the other side of the net. The toss and wrist can then be **synchronized** to have the serve dip into the box. As instructors, we should know that hitting multiple serves in the net **should not happen** and **covering** the net is a great way to consistently **clear** the net. The point I want to make is that serving double faults in **tight situations** is not only a concern for young talented teens or intermediate adults, but can sometimes be an issue for the **professional.** If all of the above fixes fail, then a sport's psychologists can be consulted in an effort to get the **subconscious** mind and the **conscious** mind to work together.

Practice, Practice, Practice: Serving in tennis is similar to shooting a **foul shot** in basketball. A lot of practice is required to become really good. As said previously I recommend **100 serves** per day, 6 days a week; not 200; not 300 but 100 serves hit to various spots in the service court. The first 25 easy and relaxed; the second 25 medium and relaxed; the last 50 should be hit with the player's full power. Keep in mind that 80% of the power is generated with the proper wrist pronation. The focus should be on hitting the **serve over the net** and in the service box to a particular spot. **Flat, slice and topspin** serves should all be practiced. It is the daily repetition that develops the required muscle memory to duplicate a particular serve in pressure situations. Hitting more than 100 serves per day increases the risk of injuring a young arm or shoulder. Serves hit in practice matches should not be included in the total of 100 serves. In practice matches all serves should be attempted regardless of whether you are winning or losing. It is only when hitting all the serves you have practiced, will you get the **match repetition** necessary to fully develop your serve.

Singles Sticks: Talented teens that hope to play national tournaments, college tennis or professional tennis should practice their serve using single sticks supplied by a knowledgeable instructor. These high level competitions will have nets that are **one to two inches higher** near the net posts. It can be very frustrating for a junior player who is playing their first national or international competition to be regularly hitting the tape when serving wide. This frustration can be easily avoided by practicing with singles sticks.

Set Ups: Remember from Chapter 1, there is **no such thing** as an easy shot in tennis. Every ball strike should be approached with total focus and concentration. A player should **look at the ball with their eyes** and **see their windows or targets with their mind**. In other words, when hitting a ground stroke from the backcourt, a player must be able to visualize the **window** over the net with their mind. When hitting a volley or overhead, the **target** should be envisioned with the mind. The creation of the proper window over the net is extremely important, particularly when attempting a passing shot **down the line**. **Errors in the n**et should be eliminated. The net player should be **forced** to make a line call or play the volley. Don't forget to recover quickly after attempting a pass.

The **match schedule** should include 5 matches per week. One loss and 4 wins is an ideal mix. When your junior talent becomes good enough to run out of local practice partners that win, it is time to step up and supply yourself as that practice partner. Instructors will sometimes think that playing players the teen can beat will not aid their progress; but the opposite is true. Playing competitors the teenager can beat will allow the pupil to experiment and practice serves and service returns in a relaxed match situation. In addition, the talented teen will learn how **to win when not playing well**. The parents of these teens will also need to be convinced of the importance of playing practice matches that can be won by their child. The ideal practice partner should be steady and a **good hustler**. The talented teen's tournament schedule should be well thought out and recommended by the instructor in consultation with the parents. A mix of local and national level tournaments is best. The talented teen should not shy away from tournaments where their own upset is a possibility. There should be **no fear in playing peers**, even ones of lesser ability. The one hour weekly lesson should include discussions and practice concerning disguise of all shots, but particularly the serve. Repaying errors should be a big part of playing practice points. A variety of overheads and swinging volleys should be practiced regularly. Weight training should be minimized, but conditioning using a teenagers own body weight encouraged. Keeping young players **free of injury** should be the number one priority. Remember that a talented player can only fully use their talent by being able to play for the **long term**. Video analysis of matches against other talented teens should be analyzed by both student and coach. This can be a tremendous learning tool for the gifted teen. Finally the talented teenager should be informed of the benefits of rest, stretching and proper nutrition. These benefits will reward the student for a lifetime.

Singles advice to talented teens: Advice given to juniors who wish to play tournament tennis and become the best singles player possible should start with the 5 C's of winning singles play. The 5 are **consistency**, **court coverage**, **concentration** and **control**. If **power** is added while maintaining the C ingredients, you have the basis for an excellent singles player. More information on the 5 C's can be found in Chapter 6, p. 71.

Cultivating a winning mindset: How does a coach help a young, talented student develop a winning mindset and why is it important in **close matches?** Players develop a winning mindset by **winning** and the more they win, the more they feel that they are **suppose to win**. It is the responsibility of the coach to select the appropriate practice partners for their students that wish to play tournament tennis. This is especially true for singles players. As stated previously, a win-loss ratio of 4-1 is approximately the right ratio to make **winning normal** for the student. These practice match **wins** should include a variety of players. This variety should include players who are lobbers, pushers and quick players who can cover the court. Practice match losses should include older, experienced players with a variety of styles. **Left-handers** should also be included in both categories.

How does a winning mindset help a player in close matches? In a close match that is winnable, a player with a winning mindset will seldom beat themselves; and since **winning is now normal,** the mind and body will most often play relaxed tennis and **avoid** those nervous moments that can spell disaster and losses.

To become a great match player, the **desire to win** must be greater than the **fear of losing.** One reason that players often resist playing practice matches with lessor players within their peer group is the fear of losing. This is especially true for talented juniors. Knowledgeable instructors must convince players that it's a big world out there and competition in your own backyard is a **valuable tool** for improvement.

Tournament Play and Manners: Great teachers should advise all juniors who wish to play tournament tennis that bad behavior will not be dignified or tolerated. This includes both on court and off court behavior. **Emotional control** while competing should be emphasized and good manners following a tournament's completion should include **thanking the tournament director** for their role as the organizer of the event. Parents should also be advised to be on their best behavior and resist the temptation to become involved in their child's match. Children should be left alone to deal with any match controversies. They should also be advised that as a **last resort**, they have the option to appeal to the tournament director. Children will learn best if they are allowed to settle all arguments over line calls, score-keeping and cheating with their opponent.

Instructors should make students aware of the possibility of unsportsmanlike conduct: Until electronic line calling becomes the norm in junior matches and college matches, disputes between competitors over line calls will continue. These conflicts are part of the human condition and while most players are honest, some are not. Line calls (particularly **service calls**) can be a huge factor in determining the outcome of a match. With two pairs of young eyes watching every close call, one would think that mistakes would be infrequent. However, disagreements over line calls can and do occur. It might be poor eyesight, nerves, or a desire to **negotiate** every call that is close. Most players view line calls as a black or white issue; the ball is either in or out. But some players want to negotiate everything from interference to lets. Even double bounces are often contested.

Experience is a great teacher when dealing with these unpleasant situations, but fair outcomes are **not guaranteed**. If you are adverse to confrontations, then you will **never** be able to successfully deal with a cheater. Cheating and bad sportsmanship are part of the game and confrontation is a necessary and warranted action. **Blatant cheating** needs to be dealt with in a **swift** and **decisive** manner and offending players need to be put on notice that this unfairness will not be tolerated. The days of saying to your opponent, "Are you sure?" are over. Remember that an integral part of your player resume is your ability to handle these disagreements. Blatant cheaters will seldom rise to the 6.0 level where matches are umpired in earnest. Every player that plays a particular cheater will have to deal with the same lack of sportsmanship. You will in part, be judged with how **you** handle these situations relative to your peers.

Once all arguments are over, the best way in dealing with line calls, interference and let disputes is to stay focused in the moment. Junior players should realize that any opponent who consistently gives bad line calls is **displaying weakness** and a lack of faith in their ability to win the match fairly. Use that to increase your concentration and to reinforce the idea that you are the better player and will prevail despite the annoyance of losing an argument over an occasional point. Regardless of the outcome of any match, juniors should **not allow** these incidents to deter them from achieving **their goals**. If you are talented enough and persistent enough, eventually your matches will be umpired. You will encounter all types of individuals in competitive tennis; some fair and great sport's people; some not so fair or nice. Keep in mind that bad behavior of any sort is an unpleasant trait of human beings and you will have to deal with this behavior as you travel through the uncertainties of life.

Who will watch you play? If you can become **consistent** when playing a match, you might enjoy the competitive aspect of tennis. If you become **consistent** and **can cover the court**, your parents may come and watch you play. If you can play **consistent, cover the court** and **move** your opponent (side to side and up and back) with **control**, people you don't know will watch you play. If you can play **consistent, cover the court, move your opponent** and do it with **power**, people will **pay** to watch you play.

Too Fast; Too Hard; Too Soon: One mistake that is commonly made by well-intentioned instructors is to **push** the talented teen physically too early. Teens who are not fully developed physically can easily **injure** themselves if they are given exercise regimens that exceed their body's limitations. A great coach will do everything possible to keep gifted teens **injury free**. In general, exercises with weights should be avoided. A limited amount of agility running, pull-ups and burpees are good exercises for **overall fitness** and are suitable for developing teens. Even mature professional players are often pushed beyond their physical limits by well-meaning trainers, which can easily can result in long-term injury.

All equipment that a gifted teen used should be evaluated by a great coach. This includes racquet choice, racquet weight, strings choice, string tension and shoes. These choices should be made in an effort to avoid injury. Introduction to **polyester string** (e.g. luxilon) should be done with care and forethought. Arm injuries can occur in athletes of any age if string tension is too tight or not the right string for a particular player. **Hybrid stringing** should be considered first. In spite of these coaching directives that are designed to avoid injuries, they can **still occur**. Rest is extremely important to give these unfortunate set-backs time to heal. A return to playing tennis should be gradual. Since competition for these players can be strenuous, a **healthy diet** should be emphasized.

Intermediate teens and preteens will gain the most benefit form one hour weekly private lessons. An emphasis should be put on the serve, ground strokes and practice points with the **student serving**. If the student has a close friend who is also an intermediate player, a semi-private lesson can be helpful since a reliable practice partner between lessons is a huge plus. The instructor should be aware of the goals of these intermediate players. Sometimes, if the goal of making a junior high or high school team is not met, a student can become discouraged to the point of wanting to quit tennis. A good teacher should be positive about the student's prospect of improvement and paint a positive outcome for next year. A slightly different practice schedule between lessons should be a part of the improvement progress. It is **crucial not to lose the interest** and enthusiasm of the preteen, since significant progress for this age group will surely take place.

Beginning teens and preteens will learn best in groups of 4 or more. The instruction will cost less and in large groups, there are plenty of available practice partners. Scoring, tennis terminology, hand-eye skills and serving should be starting points for these beginning players. Long-term interest is a desirable outcome for these young students. Praise and positive directives will yield maximum results. The **teen years** are a great age to talk about **fitness.** Fitness is an important lifetime endeavor and tennis can play an integral part. Tennis can be played for the rest of your life and will contribute to a healthy lifestyle. This simple message is a great way to promote tennis and to encourage a lifetime of healthy living. In addition, tennis is an excellent way to meet other like-minded people. The **social benefits** of tennis are unlimited and can open up friendships around the world. Tennis can and should be a sport for a **lifetime**.

What about doubles? Group lessons of 3 or 4 is an excellent time to spend a portion of the lesson time in teaching the game of doubles. Doubles is the ideal social game and most beginning and intermediate teens will have opportunities to play in doubles leagues as an adult. The overall **strategy** of doubles play in to have **fun** and **try to win.** Primary shots that are useful in carrying out this strategy are the **lob, poach** and **down the line**. Obviously serves, service return, volleys, overheads and groundstrokes are important parts of any tennis competition, but poaching, hitting into the net player's alley and the lob are particularly useful in doubles. **Communication** is also a key ingredient and can be done effectively between points, games and sets. If you and your partner have lost the first set, **something needs to change** in order to increase your chances of winning. The simplest thing to try is to trade receiving courts with your partner. This is particularly true for 3.0 and 3.5 level players. Always keep in mind that the **creation of an environment** in which your partner can play their best tennis should be the **constant goal** of a great doubles combination.

Winning doubles for intermediate adults will be detailed in chapter 6.

Chapter 6
Teaching the adult player

*A*dult Instruction involves the full range of formats that can deal with a wide range of abilities. A great instructor is also friendly and outgoing; ready to engage potential customers on a daily basis. A welcoming **attitude** towards adults can open many opportunities to expand your reach within the tennis community. It is the doorway for communication and a key for success as a teacher.

In order to **facilitate learning**, knowing something about an adult's background and occupation will give outstanding instructors some tools to formulate effective lesson plans. The big difference between adults and children is **experience.** Adults must understand why something is important to know and why consistent practice is crucial for improvement. Adults must be given the freedom to experiment with different racquets, strings and grip sizes. In other words, teachers should have different demo racquets available for adults to try. Adults should be given good reasons for improving. It might be social, physical benefits or just winning more matches. Great teachers should also be aware of how adults learn. Some may be **audio learners** and will learn best if given verbal instruction. Some may be **visual learners** and will do better if **shown how** to do something. Others might learn best by "feel". This type of learner needs the freedom to experiment and find what is best for them. Teachers must also keep the lessons **relevant.** For example spending large parts of the lesson working on the split step or skipping back sideways for the overhead may not be physically suitable for all adults. Obviously advice on nutrition should be avoided. Remember these adults are there to improve their tennis skills, not their diet. Telling a story based on your own experience, and then weaving it into the lesson plan can sometimes create an emotional connection that will facilitate learning. Also, Instructors should make the practice schedules between lessons reasonable. Most adults have jobs, families and other commitments that make large blocks of practice time unworkable.

Motivation is a key ingredient for preparing the adult for learning. The Buddhist proverb, "When the student is ready, the teacher appears." This powerful adage suggests that the proper environment will set the stage for learning. In order for this saying to become appropriate, the teacher must create the proper environment and motivation for the adult learner. Sometimes an illustration about improvement along with some **well-timed humor** is just the right formula for remarkable learning. Women who play league tennis and only play doubles form the majority of women who play on a regular basis. These players are typically 3.0 or 3.5

players who could greatly benefit from the guidance of a knowledgeable pro. The best way to achieve improvement for this category is through weekly classes consisting of 3 members on one court with the professional. Depending on the drill, the professional can be free to fill in and be the fourth player. When playing practice points, replaying errors is always a good exercise. In general the professional should **avoid hitting winners** and only play straightforward consistent tennis. This will give students the opportunity to make the errors that can then be replayed.

Although there are fewer men who play league tennis, maximum **doubles benefit** for this group is best obtained with the same format that was used for women (3 players; one court; and the professional). There are quite a few men who do **prefer** individual instruction. These men may improve their overall tennis skills, but their doubles improvement may be stalled. When giving private lessons to men who only play doubles, these lessons should be linked to doubles. Doubles at the amateur level is primarily a social game, but winning can make it more fun. Therefore strategies that allow each player to play their best should be a integral part of the instructional format. The teacher should emphasize the fundamental rules of doubles play for men and women at this level. There are **two basic rules** for winning doubles for 3.0 and 3.5 players. First, the net player should **guard their alley** and expect the down the line and they should position themselves accordingly. Second, lobs over the net player should **not happen**. The net player can guard against the lob by backing up a little and looking for the lob first. Also hitting drop shots or hitting short to frequent **lobbers** will make it more difficult for them to lob. Poaching should be introduced along with serving and net play. For league doubles play, **friends** make the best partners.

Tennis teachers should inform league players at the intermediate level that four people can see line calls differently, and that mistakes can and do occur. It might be poor eyesight, nerves, or a desire to negotiate every call that is close. Most players view line calls as a black or white issue; the ball is either in or out. But some players want to negotiate everything from interference to lets. Even double bounces are often contested. This can be annoying for beginning players, but is something all players must learn to deal with. My recommendation to players playing club doubles is to **be nice** and remember that tennis at this level should be primarily a **social experience**. Remember that you may be having **lunch** afterwards.

Great instructors, when coaching **doubles**, need to inform their students of the three components that make up first-rate doubles combinations. The three C's of excellent doubles partnerships are **camaraderie, compatibility** and **communication**.

Friendship or **camaraderie** is the foundation of a strong doubles pairing. Friends tend to have more fun and have more opportunities for success if this quality is present. It is easier for friends to discuss outcomes and suggestions for improvement if a solid **rapport** exists.

Compatibility means that both partners have similar temperaments and goals. In addition, some playing styles make for better partnerships than others. An aggressive player who is capable of hitting winners pairs nicely with a steady, consistent partner who can act as the set up player or setter. This **setter** can create opportunities for the **aggressive partner** to hit winners or finish points. While two steady players can make a formidable combination, particularly at the intermediate levels, two aggressive players tend **not** to make for good partnerships. Aggressive pairings are likely to make too many errors, especially in pressure situations. Other interesting combos are a right-handed player paired with a left-handed player or two left-handed players paired together. These two partnerships can force opposing teams to deal with different serves and different spins throughout the match and can pose a myriad of problems for opposing teams.

Communication: Once an appropriate partner is selected, communication becomes the single most important factor in accomplishing improvement, enjoyment and winning results. Communication should occur **before, during** and **after** a match. **Before** a match, a strategy should be agreed on. This can be based on weather conditions, court conditions or knowledge of an upcoming opponent. This strategy should include a plan A and a plan B. **During** a match, constant communication between points and games should include any adjustments that can be made in order to improve a team's chances of success. It is a good idea for each partner to let the other know what to expect before each point is played. Questions such as: What type of serve will the server try to hit? Does the net player plan on poaching? What shot is the receiver going to try? Based on the score, a team must constantly consider whether adjustments to their initial strategy should be made. If your team is winning, changes are not necessary. If your team is **losing**, it is crucial that the **momentum** needs to change. For intermediate players, changing the court where the receiving team returns serve is always a good adjustment to make. Keep in mind that this change can only be made after a completion of a set. Another good choice for intermediate teams is to have both players play in the back court where they can focus on **consistent tennis** and maybe trying a few more lobs. Since losing teams generally make more errors than winning teams, playing a more conservative style will give the opposition more opportunities to make errors. Changing the service order or changing ends to better deal with the sun or wind is another subtle variation that can be made. **After** the completion of a match, team members should discuss the match and isolate areas that can be improved before the next match is played. A **common blunder** that is often made by well-intentioned net players is to intercept balls hit to the middle of the court, while failing to **cover their alley**. When a team is playing one up, one back tennis, balls hit to the middle of the court can easily be covered by the player in the backcourt (normally the server or the receiver). The net player should be reminded that their number one responsibility is to **cover their alley** and secondly to cover lobs attempted over their head. Poaching or hitting balls directed toward the middle of the court should be played by the net player **only if they intend to hit a winner** or finish the point. Obviously, poaching too much risks exposing the alley (poaching two or three times a set is sufficient). Because of the difficulty in pointing out tactical blunders of this type for fear of hurting a partner's feelings, it is helpful to have a third party (preferably a qualified professional) to watch your match and make some constructive suggestions. A great coach will also stress the importance of **moving toward the net post** when poaching.

The role of the net player in **doubles** and **singles** is to **finish** points. The net player's objective is to hit winners, **not** to keep the ball in play. In one up one back doubles, the role of the back court player is to play consistent tennis and look for opportunities to hit angles, short balls and to occasionally lob the net player. Keeping the net player honest with random shots down the line is also a good tactic. Unless the net player is being specifically targeted with lobs and down the alley shots, the back court player should play approximately 80% of all points. Sometimes a net player may feel that unless he or she jumps into the point, that they are not helping their partner. In general the opposite is true. The best advice for any net player is to stay out of the way, make sure your alley is covered and protect against the lob. **Unless the net player intends to hit a winner, stay out of the way.**

Differences between professional and amateur doubles: Since the majority of adult players that play doubles are intermediates, these adults hopefully will recognize that their skill level is far below the professional doubles player. Since many intermediate players watch the professionals play on **television**, there is a tendency to copy what they see. What they see are very active net players who hit lots of winners and seem to be involved in almost every point. As discussed above, amateur players should cover their alley and protect against the lob **first**. When an amateur intercepts a ball at net, a winner should result. If the net player feels that they will be unable to finish, then they should stay out of the way and **let their partner play.** Professional players, after communicating with their serving partner, will both know where the serve is going and the intention of the net player.

So far we have only discussed instruction for intermediate players who play in leagues. What about the **beginning** adult who wants to play in a league? What about the adult who wants to play with his or her spouse? What about couples who wish to play with their neighbors? These players are best served (no pun intended) with group instruction. Large groups can give each student numerous potential practice partners and enlarge their contacts with those who want to learn tennis. Some adults may have **self-doubt** about their prospects of improving and feel like they are too old to learn a new skill. This false and negative concept should be **erased** by the instructor during the first meeting. This can be done by giving examples of adult beginners who have achieved considerable improvement after beginning in a group lesson. Since practice between lessons is such an important part of progress its value should be made clear to all students.

Singles advice to adults: Advice given to adults who wish to play tournament tennis and become the best singles player possible should start with the 5 C's of winning singles play. The 5 are **consistency**, **court coverage**, **concentration** and **control**. If **power** is added while maintaining the 5 C ingredients, you have the basis for an excellent singles player.

Consistency is the single most important ingredient for being a successful tennis competitor. To be a consistent player means more than just being able to hit 100 balls in a row against a wall without missing, or to rally with a practice partner 100 times in a row. To be consistent means that a player can play with very few unforced errors against a variety of opponents and under a **variety of conditions**. A consistent player must be able to play against aggressive styles, left-handers, lobbers, pushers and still make very few errors. Also, a consistent player must be able to play in hot weather, windy conditions and high elevations while continuing to play mostly error-free tennis.

Court coverage: In order to enjoy the greatest benefit from consistent play, a tennis competitor must be able to cover the court. To have natural speed and/or quickness is a good start, but other qualities are needed to maximize court coverage. **Proper positioning** is a good place to start. For example, when receiving serve, the receiver must take a position that allows returning serve with a **minimum of movement** to the outside. Since the wide serve will pull the receiver off the court, this can open up the court for an easy winner by the server. The receiver should be able to have a good swing at any wide serves. Serves hit down the T might have to be returned at full stretch, but the receiver will be in the **middle** of the court and well positioned to begin the point. In general, a player should **mirror** their opponent's position. If your opponent is in the middle you should be in the middle. If your opponent is to your left you should be to your right. If your opponent is to your right, you should be to your left. Great court coverage also means that you should overplay or **anticipate** your opponent's **favorite shots.** Some players who are fast and extremely quick can often tire as the match wears on. To combat this, players need to make sure they are in **peak condition** so they can be at their best down the stretch where the winner is determined.

Concentration is required to be both consistent and to cover the court well. Forgetting the past and focusing on the present is the key component for consistent play and a winning style. Because the road to victory can be "paved with many potholes", particularly in a closely-contested match, a player must be able to successfully navigate the ups and downs of a tennis match. One area that can often interfere with one's concentration is determining whether a ball is in or out. **Cheating, line calling and lack of sportsmanship** can upset the focus of many a player. Until all amateur matches are umpired by *Hawk-Eye Live* or similar, disputes between adult competitors over lines calls will continue. These conflicts are an unpleasant part of the game and is something that all tennis competitors will have to deal with. This may be the first time adults have entered a competitive sport where the opponents umpire everything and line **calls** are the responsibility of you and your rival. Unfortunately, bad line calls can determine the winner of a close match. In a match with honest adults watching the lines, one would think that mistakes would seldom occur. However, even two honest adults can see the line calls differently. Squabbles over line calls will occasionally occur. This can be annoying, but is something that players at all amateur levels must **learn to deal with**. Repeating advice that was given to juniors in chapter 5, the best way in dealing with disputes over line calls or interference is to stay focused in the moment. Adults must realize that opponents who gives bad line calls are **displaying weakness** and a lack of faith in their ability to win the match fairly. Use that to increase your **concentration** and to reinforce the idea that you are the better player and will prevail despite the annoyance of losing an argument over an occasional point. Regardless of the outcome of any match, adult tournament players should **not allow** these incidents to deter them from achieving **their goals**. If you are talented enough and persistent enough, eventually your matches will be umpired. In the meantime, you will encounter all types of individuals in competitive tennis; some fair and great sport's people; some not so fair or nice. Keep in mind that **bad behavior** of any sort is a trait of some in our society and you will have to deal with this behavior as you travel through the **uncertainties of life**. **Other factors** that can hinder concentration are delays (e.g. rain delays), scheduling changes, or unfavorable court assignments. Additionally, in order to **maintain** long-term concentration, **proper hydration** before, during and after a match is crucial for consistent mental focus.

Depth and Control allows a player to establish favorable **court positions**. The ability to move an opponent side to side and up and back is a valuable tool for playing winning tennis. **Control** of one's **emotions** is also a must in order to navigate through the ups and downs of a tennis match.

Adding Power: The addition of **power** can propel an adult player to another level of competitive play. Practicing with a focus of adding power to the serve and forehand should be added without sacrificing the 5 C's. Adding **power** to the **serve** can be accomplished by regularly hitting the serve as hard as possible against a wall while trying to hit the **center** of the racquet. Adding power to the **forehand** will require practice on a ball machine with an emphasis on relaxing the arm and wrist as the ball is slapped as hard as possible. Referring to the numerous videos online of the **modern forehand** can help in this area.

Advanced adults who play tournament tennis will often want **playing lessons** with the pro. This format will give the professional an opportunity to analyze a student's strengths and weaknesses in a match simulation. Suggestions can then be conveyed to the student along with practice exercises between lessons. However, there are some exercises that are best performed with the aid of a qualified instructor. The student hitting the approach shot with the instructor attempting a pass is a valuable sequence to practice. The student should be informed of the direction of the attempted pass, so that the proper anticipation can be practiced. Overheads and winning volleys are shots that are typically under-practiced even among advanced players.

Don't forget the singles sticks: As indicated in Chapter 5 for talented juniors, the net will be one to two inches higher when serving wide in top level competition. Therefore, in preparation for a national championship, adults should practice their serve using singles sticks.

Cultivating a winning mindset: How does a coach help a motivated talented adult develop a winning mindset and why is it important in **close matches?** As discussed in chapter 5 with the talented junior player, adults also need the proper direction to develop this winning mindset. We know that players develop this mindset by winning and the more they win, the more they feel that they are **supposed to win**. It is the responsibility of the coach to select the appropriate practice partners for these adults that wish to play tournament tennis. This is especially true for singles players. A win-loss ratio of 4-1 is approximately the right ratio to make **winning normal** for the student. These practice match **wins** should include a variety of players. This variety should include players who are lobbers, pushers and quick players who can cover the court. Practice match losses should include experienced players with a variety of styles. **Left-handers** should also be included in both categories.

How does the winning mindset help an adult player in a close match? In a close match that is winnable, a player with a winning mindset will seldom beat themselves; and since **winning will now be normal,** the mind and body will most often play relaxed tennis and **avoid** those nervous moments that can spell disaster and losses. Double faults and unforced errors will be minimized in these critical moments of a tightly contested match. A winning mindset will **not help** a player when they are **overmatched**, but can be an enormous help in winnable matches and close contests. Obviously, adult tournament players can profit from playing practice matches with players of **all ages.**

Adults need to be reminded that in order to become a great match player, the **desire to win** must be greater than the **fear of losing.** One reason that players often resist playing practice matches with lessor players within their peer group is the **fear of losing**. Knowledgeable instructors must convince all players that it's a big world out there and competition in your own backyard is a **valuable tool** for improvement.

Team practices for intermediates are sometimes desired by league captains and other team members. These practices with 8 or more students can be of benefit when under the direction of an outstanding pro. Payments can be collected in advance for a set number of practices. This will lower costs and should boost attendance. Drills can be suggested and analysis can be given to team members as a group. This will ensure that each team member is on the same page and will promote interest in everyone's results. Instructors must be creative when an odd number of students turn up. In order to maximize improvement, several courts may be required when performing each drill. A great instructor will stay abreast of the team's results and **recognize and praise** any improvement. A weekly team practice during the league season should result in real progress.

Important Shots and Points: When playing a **point**, the most important **shot** is the next one. When playing a **game**, the most important **point** is the next one and when playing a **set** the most important **game** is the next one. Note that the past, which cannot be changed, should be forgotten. Every great player must have a **short memory**. Since the **past is a statement** and the **future is a question mark**, playing in the **present** is the key for playing your best tennis. In addition, you **can** and **must** control your emotions in order to have consistent success when **competing** in a tennis match. The reader should reread this paragraph to ensure that the entire meaning is understood. It is well known that **Momentum is** a huge factor in sports, particularly tennis: Even though good and bad streaks will surely happen and likely determine the winner, an effort should be made to maintain your level of play during good streaks and to change things up during a bad streak. Eight points or more in a row or five games in a row are **streaks** that generally determine match outcomes.

Senior players can make up the most enjoyable part of the instructor's teaching schedule. Seniors and super seniors (over 75 years of age) are typically eager to try new things in an effort to improve. Their improvement expectations are generally lower and they can give valuable feedback that can help instructors with other age groups. Since senior players are blessed with experience their feedback can be significant. Some of the same principles revealed in chapter 2 apply to this demographic. **Having fun** and **no injuries is the goal.** Seniors are less likely to swing their racquet and hit someone than 4-6 year-olds, but their can get hurt in other ways. Tripping over loose balls, muscle pulls, stroke and heat exhaustion are all common traumas that instructors must be prepared for.

When giving lessons outdoors to seniors in a **hot climate**, water should be nearby and readily available. Dehydration is often the cause of a heat-related illness. If you suspect a senior is suffering from heat exhaustion, find shade and immediately place a wet towel around the victim's neck and encourage the drinking of water or a sports drink. Heat exhaustion can lead to **heat stroke** which is a medical emergency. A knowledgeable teacher should know the difference. Hot moist skin, nausea, loss of consciousness and vomiting are signs of heat stroke and 911 should be called.

Loose balls on the court can lead to falls and broken bones for the senior player. A good teacher must be aware of balls that pose a danger for those receiving instruction. Windy outdoor conditions can cause balls to move while drills are in progress. Muscle pulls are common among seniors. A gentle warm-up is recommended. Warming up with short court rallies is a nice gentle exercise for getting the muscles warm and the hand-eye coordination sharpened. This is an ideal time to emphasize watching the ball and hitting the center of the racquet. The preceding advice is useful for all age groups, but is especially valuable for seniors. A good instructor recognizes that seniors are typically set in their ways as far as technique, but will readily accept advice on strategy and tactics. The **drop shot** and the **lob** gradually become offensive weapons as a player ages. Teachers can mistakenly think that since the answer to the lob is the overhead, that overhead practice for seniors will eliminate the frequency of the lob. The lob is a touch shot and requires little in the way of practice. The overhead however, requires agility, timing and eye-hand skills that slowly deteriorate with aging. The best advice for combatting the frustration of dealing with a lobber is to **learn the drop shot**. If a player can force the opposition to come to net, then an opponent's lob response ceases to be a good option. Some seniors may erroneously think that hitting harder with more topspin is the answer, but this is seldom the case and can easily result in more errors. The best time to drop shot is on your opponent's **second serve**. The receiver not only has a short ball but the server starts at the baseline. When receiving the second serve, the receiver's top options are in order the drop shot, lob over the net player and down the net player's alley. All options should be discussed and practiced in the lesson format. When an error is made, the teacher can decide if the replay of the error is warranted.

Racquet Selection: The proper racquet for the senior player can make a big difference. In general, a larger racquet head will give seniors a larger sweet spot and allow for greater ball control and power. Since the swing speed of the senior player slows with age, the extra power a larger face provides should be apparent, particularly on the serve. The string tension should be about 5 – 10 pounds lower than the manufacturers recommended. This will not only provide more power but will be easier on the arm and shoulder. Softer strings such as gut and some nylons should also be considered. Polyester strings **should be avoided**. Even though most of the top professionals use polyester strings such as "luxilon", it is a stiff string and to the average senior can seem unresponsive. Since the top pros are able to generate extremely fast swing speeds, they are able to generate tremendous topspin with the smooth surface of the polyester string. If tennis elbow is a persistent problem for the senior, a slightly larger grip can reduce some pressure on the elbow.

Playing tennis is also a great way to augment the **flexibility** of seniors. An insightful instructor can enhance this important aspect of a senior's physical condition by instituting some simple stretches as part of the instructional content. A good way to start each session is to have all participants, including the instructor to reach for the sky and take a deep breath; hold for 10 seconds and release. Some easy neck rolls and side bends are a nice addition. After practicing some short court, serving is a nice way to begin the instructional part of each lesson. Many seniors who have played tennis for the majority of their life are stuck in technique patterns that are difficult to change. Technique changes that don't yield immediate results are generally discarded by the time the next lesson occurs. Since a significant portion of seniors tend to hit down on the ball when serving, the following service warm-up exercises, which are designed to hit up and over the ball and may allow for instant technique improvement while increasing **flexibility.**

In addition greater margin when serving can be achieved. Have your senior student hit two serves easy and then two serves medium **over the net** and in the box. While swinging easy and loose, then try to hit four serves over the baseline and then four against the fence. Lastly, trying to hit four serves over the back fence will help add power to the serve and at the same time increase the flexibility of the trunk. In this portion of the lesson, a great instructor must be aware of any limitations that a senior player may have, so that **injury can be avoided**. It should be emphasized that the service motion must be **nice and loose**. After this service warm-up phase, the emphasis should be put on consistency and net clearance; easy and medium serves are recommended. Hitting the serve hard can be done later in the lesson, when playing practice points. The middle portion of the lesson should focus on drop shots, winning volleys and overheads. The instructor should be the feeder when practicing volleys and overheads. **Balance, solid contact and placement** should be underscored. The instructor should make every attempt to allow the student to hit easy overheads and volleys.

Special cases: Sometimes you might encounter a 75+ year-old who has played their entire life and just wants to hit with someone who can hit the ball to them. Some seniors may want to play points only while having the opportunity to move the instructor around. The instructor **should not** try to move the senior player around as this might risk injury. These seniors do not want or need instruction, but merely want to play. These players give a creative instructor many ways to increase the enjoyment of both the senior and the instructor. As my dear friend and fellow USPTA pro Hugh Waters used to say; **"To play is to win."**

Learning can have multiple benefits for seniors: Seniors can benefit both physically and mentally by gaining a sense of accomplishment when actively involved in doing something new. Many super seniors have calendars that are filled with doctor's appointments, but little else. Having a weekly tennis lesson can be a nice break and give them something to look forward to. Also, learning new tennis skills and strategies can encourage seniors to develop and **maintain** social connections. This can help with self-confidence while improving the quality of their life. Multiple studies have concluded that when seniors are involved in learning activities that promote **social interaction,** depression due to social isolation can be prevented.

§ *Team Coaching* §

Chapter 8
Grade School

*P*articipation, learning and fun are the **principle ingredients** of any successful grade school program. Parents who play tennis should be recruited to coach individual teams while the tennis professional organizes the league format, number of teams and schedule.

Funds are crucial in the initial planning: Many of these players will need racquets and teams will need tennis balls for practice and matches. Professional organizations such as the USPTA, USTA and USPTR are all potential sources of funds. Local businesses, United Way and some charities can also be great funding assets. Racquets and balls need not be new.

Promotion in Individual Grade Schools: Clinics and exhibitions given by the tennis professional are an **integral part** of any Grade School League program. Exhibitions should consist of music, prizes, student participation and anything that brings **excitement** to youngsters in grades 1 – 6. I know of one talented professional that gave 15 exhibitions over 4 days to an average crowd of 400 students. This type of promotion will require the cooperation of the local School Board and teachers. Printed promotional material can be given to individual principals for student signup and start dates. Depending on skill level grades 1-3 could make up the JV team and grades 4-6 the varsity.

Newspaper Role: Publicity will be important for these young beginning tennis players. Small notices such as matches played and the names of individual students participating will also help the local newspaper sell their product. Weekly standings listing the participating Grade Schools will help promote the League and increase visibility. Everyone likes to see their name in the newspaper and the local professional can organize these notices to make it easy on the local sports reporters. The knowledgeable pro also recognizes a successful grade school league can be of great benefit to his business.

What about Practices? One practice per week along with one team match per week should sufficient. The serve; singles and doubles match play and scoring should be emphasized in practice. Depending on skill level, 8 & under may be allowed to serve from the service line. Practice and match length should be restricted to no more than 90 minutes.

Have parents promote and share standings on Facebook and other social media. The more publicity the better. This publicity might encourage other parents to start their own League. The building of new tennis courts on school property could give a tremendous boost to tennis participation. **Is everyone allowed to play?** The short answer is yes. All players regardless of ability or knowledge should be allowed to participate. A **positive learning experience** is the goal. Returning young players will show great improvement after a season of involvement and becoming a year older.

What about 11 and 12-year-olds that have had tournament experience? Absolutely, they should be allowed and encouraged to participate. These players can raise the level of all players just by being part of the team. The more of these accomplished players that are part of the League, the better. Some of these players have been exposed to private coaches and many will probably enjoy a change of venue. The opportunity to socialize with their peer group cannot be overstated. Developing players for a lifetime of tennis enjoyment is the objective, not only at this age but for all age groups.

Rules: Since Grade Schools Leagues will be made up of 6 thru 12-year-olds, including children with a wide range of tennis ability, **flexibility** is the key ingredient for a successful program. Decisions on rules, scoring, format and team scores should be made by a qualified professional. Even season-ending awards should be made with the sensitivity of the child a priority. Small participation awards like vibration dampeners, certificates or baggage tags make suitable kudos for a season well-done. Some tennis professional may be willing to give a free clinic to all participants as a way of promoting their own programs.

T-shirts for all players: Another way to promote tennis and participating Grade Schools is to have T-shirts given to all players. Funds can be raised by parents or there may be businesses in the area that will donate T-shirts in exchange for their name or logo on the shirt-sleeve. The school name and mascot (e.g. Busy Creek Grade School) could be displayed on the shirt front. Individual names of players need not be on school's T-shirt, since the **team aspect** should be emphasized. All coaches should remember that this should be a fun league designed to educate.

What about tennis courts? Most grade schools do not have their own tennis courts. However, if land is available, building courts on school property is an option that will need School Board and community support. The professional should check with nearby junior highs and high schools to see if their courts might be available at off times for practices and matches. Local community colleges might also be an option.

End of season: Let teachers and administration know about plans for the following year. **Hats** given to players to promote next year's league can be a nice touch. Remember that **fun** is required in order to produce players that will play for a lifetime.

Chapter 9
Junior High (Middle School)

Participation, **competition** and fun are also the **principle ingredients** of all successful Junior High programs. In addition, a definite league structure plus the **completive nature** of tennis should begin to emerge. Hopefully county and state leagues already exist. This will make starting a program at an individual school easier. Teachers at these participating schools should be recruited to coach. These teachers should be paid a **stipend** for their service. Physical education instructors are a good place to start. Ideally these teachers will be paid a stipend by the school district. Existing leagues make for an easy transition, since individual schools programs can be copied. If the current league has coaches that are not paid by the school district, fund raising efforts should be started so that all coaches can receive some monetary compensation for their time and effort. Local tennis professionals can be recruited to help and promote an all-out-effort to form new school teams. This will help their business and increase player numbers.

Organized practices: Practices should consist primarily of challenge matches, service and service return drills and tie-breaker round robins. Assuming courts are available, JV (junior varsity) teams should be a part of any successful junior high programs. The **more players** the better.

Consistency: Team practices provide an excellent opportunity for improving the overall consistency of grade school, junior high or high school players. Great coaches recognized that consistent players tend to win matches and error prone players tend to lose matches. Coaches can institute a simple drill that will not only improve each player's consistency, but will promote team unity. The drill is simply this: Two players try to keep the ball in play for a count of 50 hits (25 for each player). The ball can only bounce once and has to be inside the singles lines. The coach must convince each player, regardless of ability, the importance of striving for this 50 count goal. Top players may only want to hit with teammates of comparable talent. However, the coach must convince the entire squad of the benefit to both the individual and the team in attempting this drill involving all skill levels. There is a tendency to blame the less skillful player for the majority of misses. This tendency obscures the entire purpose of the drill. The more **advanced** players need to recognize that they play the **major** role in achieving the 50 count goal. The advanced players on the team must be able to temper their shots so that the beginning players have a reasonable chance for success. Contrary to popular opinion, this will **not have a detrimental effect** on the advanced player's development, but will likely improve the touch, feel and judgment of everyone. Advanced players may rebel doing this exercise if they are forced to do it for too long or too often. The coach must be aware when this drill becomes stale. In general, 10 to 15 minutes is **sufficient** to maximize improvement.

In order for this simple drill to achieve **maximum benefit**, players should try to be near the baseline on the majority of shots. Players who quickly execute 50 shots, can advance to using only the backhand; then only the forehand. High school players should be able to alternate forehand and backhand and then topspin and slice. Depending on the number of courts, this exercise can be done on a single court with two, three, four or five players. Grade school players might need to play short court first (having the bounce inside the service boxes), before advancing to the baseline.

Who plays and in what position? Positions should be based on challenge matches. Challenge matches are best held weekly and should consist of one set with a 7-point tie-breaker at 6-6. Round robin tie-breakers are also a great way to determine player position.

Why should teaching professionals get involved? A great tennis professional, who is an artist and makes use of the current scientific methods, needs eager students to pass along his or her expertise and produce insightful players of all ages and talent levels. Junior high programs are a **critical** part of that scenario. The tennis professional can then become an integral part in producing individuals that love the game of tennis and will play for a lifetime.

Chapter 10
High School

$\mathcal{T}$he high school coach must be involved in the recruitment of players of all levels. Talented players who may have a state or national ranking may **be reluctant** to play high school tennis, if they feel it may interfere with their training. They also may feel they are too good or not really wanted by the coach or their peer group. The coach must reassure the prospective player that accommodations can be made for their training and tournament schedule. Also the encouragement of classmates can greatly assist in the recruitment process. It is the responsibility of a great coach to actively recruit these players and let them know that they are **wanted and needed**.

Recommended Weekly Practice Schedule (Sample): Two hour practices; five days/week (off season)

Monday – Primary focus; <u>challenge matches and tie-breaker round robins</u>

>   **Stretch and loosen up.** (5 minutes)

>   **Matches** (115 minutes) – 8 game pro-sets; tie-breaker at 7-7

Tuesday – Primary focus; <u>serving, service return and transition play</u>

>   **Stretch and loosen up.** (5 minutes)

>   **Jog the lines**; refer to pp. 99-100 (5 minutes)

>   **Serve** – each player hits 60 serves, 30 ad court, and 30 deuce court. Changes ends after 30 serves (30 minutes)

>   **Transition play** – two servers, one receiver; when server wins 3 points in a row, sever becomes receiver (90 minutes)

Wednesday – Primary focus; <u>consistency from the backcourt</u>

>   **Stretch and loosen up.** (5 minutes)

>   **Jog the lines**; refer to pp. 99-100 (5 minutes)

>   **Practice the following** – rally with partner; 50 shots without missing. Then 50 shots forehand only; then 50 backhand only; then 50 alternating forehand and backhand. Change partners and ends regularly. (110 Minutes)

Thursday – Primary focus; doubles

> **Stretch and loosen up.** (5 minutes)

> **Jog the lines**; refer to pp. 99-100 (5 minutes)

> **Play doubles** – experiment with different teams; emphasize poaching, protecting your alley first and the power of the **lob**. Encourage communication and the creating of a proper environment for maximum results and enjoyment. Change sides often to negate effects of sun and wind. (110 minutes)

Friday – Primary focus; lobs, overheads and drop shots

> **Stretch and loosen up.** (5 minutes)

> **Jog the lines**; refer to pp. 99-100 (5 minutes)

> **Lobs, overheads and drop shots** – types of practice depend on ability of team

Injuries: Remember, a coach must do everything within reason to keep a team **injury free.** That requires a constant **vigilance** of all drills and practice matches by the coach. A player's choice of racquets and string selection should be understood by the coach. Doing repetition (e. g. heavy hitting from the backcourt) in windy conditions should be avoided.

Unsuitable stringing is the most common way that high school players can acquire an injury that will leave them unable to perform. Wrist and arm injuries caused by ill-suited racquet stringing can wreak havoc on a young player's future. Strings that are too tight or too stiff may wear well, but can be tough on young arms and cause serious injury requiring lengthy periods of rest and rehab. For some, **cost** can be the primary factor in string selection, while the stress this choice puts on a young arm is **neglected**.

Loose tennis balls that are accidently **stepped on** while practicing. Sprained ankles and twisted knees can be the gruesome result. This can easily occur in windy conditions where balls are rolling around behind players who are focused on playing a point or hitting a shot.

Improper use of weights: Weight training is often counter-productive when training for tennis. Agility drills (e. g. jogging the lines) are best for improving the court coverage of all players. Service improvement and practicing shots that finish points are the best way for **quick** players to progress.

Excessive running: Agility drills such as jogging or running the lines should be the preferred types of conditioning. Distance running should be avoided. Even a mile distance is of very little benefit in a sport that puts a premium on **flexibility and quickness.**

Chapter 11
College

*C*ollege coaching requires an individual to have outstanding people skills and to be an expert recruiter. This individual must also be capable of dealing with players from different countries, different cultures and be able to successfully navigate the **competitive environment** that is college tennis. Not only is the college coach asked to guide young people in their pursuit of tennis excellence, but the coach must require **excellence in the classroom**. A cooperative administration is fundamental in having a great program and it is the responsibility of the coach to forge the proper channels of communication when dealing with athletic directors, presidents and professors. A successful college tennis program needs to be **properly funded** and have the facilities necessary to recruit, practice and play their home schedule. These requirements must be made clear to athletic directors and all those making financial decisions involving the tennis program.

An additional responsibility of the coach is to field the best players in order of ability and to keep players **healthy**. This is especially important when preparing for championship tournaments or important team matches. Many coaches can be **overly concerned** about harmony among their players; particularly very competitive players. The coach who wants to ensure that animosity among players concerning position is eliminated might be tempted to rank players according to past results or by observing their play in practice. This **concern** can sometimes override the appropriate selection process and create a negative energy within the team. So then, how should this selection process be done? The obvious answer is to have regular challenge matches to determine team rank.

Imagine this scenario. You have a **championship team** with all players returning including the NCAA Division I singles champion plus a three-time All-American. In addition you have an incoming freshman who has just lost in the semi-finals at Wimbledon joining the team. Obviously all players are extremely competitive. How then would you determine team rank? Having the current **NCAA singles champ** and the **Wimbledon semi-finalist** on the same team could present a selection problem if team members felt that the selection process was unfair.

[11] This scenario was the situation that legendary Stanford coach **Dick Gould** was presented with in the fall of 1977. Eighteen-year-old incoming freshman **John McEnroe** had just lost to Jimmy Connors in the semifinal at Wimbledon in four sets. Gould also had the defending NCAA singles champion **Matt Mitchell** plus two outstanding returning players, Perry Wright and Bill Maze. So how

did this legendary coach determine the rank of his players? He had the entire team play a round robin during team practices and on the basis of these results, ranked the first four players in this order (1. McEnroe, 2. Maze, 3. Perry Wright, 4. Matt Mitchell). Surprisingly, the defending NCAA singles champ, Matt Mitchell was ranked fourth. Gould knew he had a very competitive team. The players were so competitive that he worried the team might implode before the season was over. [12] They did not however, and finished the regular season at 24-0. They defeated UCLA 6-3 in the team finals and McEnroe, on a hot, humid afternoon, secured the NCAA singles title by defeating North Carolina State's John Sadri 7-6, 7-6, 5-7, 7-6.

Student First, Athlete Second: A collegiate tennis player must pass his or her coursework in order to stay in school and to participate on the tennis team. An astute coach will stress the importance of good grades to all team members and will attempt to develop a rapport with a variety of professors who might teach his or her team members. Sitting in the **first row** and attending **class regularly** is always good advice to give to any student athlete. The vast majority of college tennis players will **never** make a living **playing** tennis. A **select few** may make a living **teaching** tennis. Because of this sobering reality, a college tennis player needs to prepare for a life **after college tennis**. The best way to accomplish a smooth transition to life after tennis is to obtain a college degree by taking and passing courses designed to increase a player's **opportunities** for an enjoyable life.

Conditioning: The college coach should be well versed in **all aspects** of the conditioning program. Too often tennis teams are subjected to a strength and weight program developed by trainers that oversee all of the college's athletic programs. These trainers can sometimes excel in training football players or athletes where strength is a primary attribute required for excellence. These programs often fall short in training tennis players. Tennis requires **flexibility** and many tennis players entering college have never lifted weights in earnest. Knowing how to **properly stretch**, particularly after tennis practice or after matches is the key to improving flexibility, recovery and avoiding **injuries.** While improving one's strength and power is important for all athletes including tennis players, a weight program should not sacrifice flexibility for strength. **Jogging** the lines under control before practice is a nice warm-up. The forward, backward and sideways movement massages the joints and increases blood flow to the legs and feet. **Running** the lines for time (twice on each side of the net) several times a week will greatly improve endurance and agility.

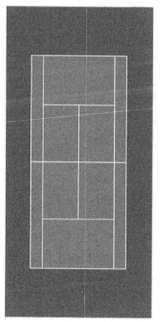

Fig 1

Running the Lines (Description): In figure 1, starting at the lower left hand corner where the doubles line intersects the baseline, a player moves sideways along the baseline to the right hand corner and runs forward along the doubles line to the net and touches. Player then retraces the outside line for doubles by running backwards to the baseline, then sideways to the intersection of the baseline and singles line, then runs forward and touches the net, then backwards to the intersection of the singles line and service line, then sideways to the center service line and then forward to the net. Player then runs backwards to the service line, then sideways to the singles line, then forward to the net, then backwards to the baseline, then sideways to the doubles line and runs forward to the net, then backwards to baseline which brings the player back to the original starting position (counts as running the lines once). The player repeats and returns to the starting point (player has now run the lines twice). Player then runs around the net post to the other side and retraces the lines twice more. If jogging a college player should complete the course in about **4 minutes**. If running, **2 minutes 20 seconds** is good. A world class athlete might be able to complete course in about **2 minutes**.

Additional Recommended Conditioning: Push-ups, pull-ups and burpees are excellent exercises that stretch and pull abdominals under tension. These exercises uses one's own body weight and should be done with the correct form to maximize their benefit.

Drills and the Ball Machine: An investment in 2 or 3 good ball machines should allow for multiple drills that emphasize beginning and ending points. Serves and service return (the two most important shots in tennis) should be practiced with team members doing both the serving and receiving. A serving ball machine such as the "Ace Attack" are excellent for practicing only service returns. Playing sets while serving from the "T" will help players to disguise their serves. This exercise of serving from the "T" will also allow practice on net play since server will be forced to play the net (particularly good for counter-punchers and backcourt players).

Don't forget to practice the drop shot and to **remind players that the drop shot should not be used against players that are faster than the one hitting the drop shot, especially on big points.** Sometimes coaches will spend the majority of practice time having their players rally from the back court. While some practice on ground strokes (particularly the **transition** following serving) can be helpful, too much time spent on just rallying from the backcourt (e.g. starting the rally with a ground stroke), can take away from valuable practice time that could be spent on the **more important** shots of **serving, receiving** and **finishing points.**

Travel: A wise coach knows the stress involved in travel which can put an unnecessary burden on a young person's physical and mental condition, particularly when traveling through time zones. Even **professional players** can and do experience "jet lag" and other travel related issues in going from tournament to tournament. The following is a good example of the possible negative effects of excessive travel. The 2021 US Open Women's Single Champion, the teen-age sensation Emma Raducanu, certainly had her work cut out for her by traveling from New York in mid-September to London and then to Indian Wells, CA to play in the *BNP Paribus Open* in October. After receiving a wild card and a first round bye, she proceeded to lose to the number 100 player in the world 6-2, 6-4 on October 9th. Emma had traveled through 5 time zones in traveling from New York to London and then 8 time zones in going from London to Indian Wells all in less than a month. A 6-2, 6-4 opening round loss was not surprising. Emma's **tentative** schedule for the rest of 2021 is **brutal**. She has plans to play the Kremlin Cup in Moscow, October 18-24, the Transylvania Open in Romania, October 25-31, then the WTA Finals in Guadalajara Mexico, November 8-14 (elevation 5200 feet), then an exhibition in Abu Dhabi, December 16-18, followed by the Australian Open which begins on January 17, 2022. In Australia she may have to quarantine for two weeks before she can practice ahead of the Australian Open.

Another example is world number one Novak Djokovic's attempt to win the "Golden Slam" (All four Grand Slams and the Olympic gold all in the same calendar year). After winning the Wimbledon final on July 11th, Novak traveled from London to Tokyo (**8 time zones**) to play in the Olympic Games which started on July 24th. After losing to Alex Zevrev in the quarterfinals, he traveled to New York (**13 time zones**) to play in the US Open. Novak had traveled through **21 time zones** in less than 2 months. Loses in the Olympics and the US Open were not surprising when viewed thru the "travel lens".

Elevation changes can also wreak havoc on a player's ability to produce their best tennis. The **Mountain West Conference** (MWC) is a good example of what some teams may experience in playing matches at different elevations. The elevation of the tennis courts at the Air Force Academy is approximately 7200 feet above sea level and at San Diego State University approximately 400. It can take tennis players one or two weeks to adjust to playing at a seven thousand feet elevation difference. **High altitude balls** and the thin air at elevations above 3500 feet require a period of adjustment that most college players are not given the luxury of attaining. One such player that was forced to deal with some extreme elevation changes during his 4-year college career was a young Air Force cadet named **Shannon Buck**. In addition to being the MWC player of the year in 2006, Shannon was a **2-time All-American** at the Air Force Academy and a 4-time MWC selection. Buck was the only player in Air Force Academy history to qualify for two NCAA Championships and according to two ex-coaches was without question, the **greatest tennis player** in Academy history. In a phone interview with Shannon on October 30, 2021, I asked Shannon about the adjustments of playing at different elevations during his college career. "When I first qualified for the NCAA Championships in 2003, the tournament was held in Athens, GA (approx. 700 feet above sea level). It felt as if I was playing in unusually heavy air with lively balls that I couldn't seem to hit past the service line. Needless to say, I didn't play my best tennis."

Transition following Serving should be practiced: In order to practice transitioning from serving to playing a point to its conclusion, two players should play each other in **singles** until the server wins four points. After winning four points the server becomes the receiver and play continues until the receiver wins four points. Then both players should change sides and repeat. This can also be done in **doubles**. This transition practice is important in order to develop the **smooth change in rhythm** required to avoid needless errors after serving or receiving. In other words, shots practiced in isolation, although important, transition practice can smoothly incorporate the variety of shots needed to successfully compete to the best of one's ability.

Healthy Living: Young athletes need to hear words of wisdom from a coach that will direct them toward a healthy lifestyle. Obviously, smoking and drinking will negatively affect a tennis player's performance and will **not** lead to a healthy lifestyle. Young competitive athletes need to hear from the coach that **drinking and smoking are the enemy** of any serious athlete. In addition, some good advice concerning nutrition is crucial for peak performance. Some clear-cut advice regarding proper food choices should focus on a wide variety of leafy greens, vegetables, fruits, legumes, nuts and grains. While avoiding foods that are high in sugar, salt and fat.

Players should also avoid saturated fats and trans-fatty acids. There is **no need** to promote weight reduction. Young athletes can be very sensitive about their body image, so promoting healthy food choices is the best way to influence players toward a healthy lifestyle.

Positive Visualization: In the same way that practicing tennis will program our subconscious mind to produce consistency when playing a match, mentally preparing before a match can also program our subconscious in a positive way. **Great coaches** recognize the importance of the **subconscious mind** and how it relates to the conscious mind when playing a competitive tennis match. If we reflect on some of the ideas presented in chapter two, we might recall some of the differences between the conscious and subconscious mind. For example, the first time we learned to drive a stick shift, the **conscious mind** had to work extremely hard to successfully coordinate the clutch, gas pedal and gear shift in order to accomplish a smooth driving experience. With sufficient practice, driving a stick shift became automatic and the subconscious took over. Remember that the subconscious mind is your computer and has made a record of everything that has happened in your life to date. It has also recorded your fears, likes, dislikes, goals, dreams and every thought that you have ever had. The subconscious mind is **non-judgmental**. It will only tell your conscious mind in an impartial and unfiltered way what it has recorded. Your subconscious mind wants to work with your conscious mind and gets **nervous** when your conscious mind wants to proceed without it. **What do I mean by nervous?** Your subconscious mind controls all your involuntary bodily functions, like breathing, blood pressure and heart rate. Many other actions associated with one's nervous system are also controlled by the subconscious mind. However, the conscious mind only works in **the present** and can only look into a somewhat biased version of the **future**. You might think that your conscious mind can control the subconscious, but in fact the opposite is true. Every time your conscious mind wants to do something, it will check with your subconscious to see if it is permitted. For example, if for fun your conscious mind decides on a dare to jump from the top of a twenty story building, your conscious mind will ask your subconscious if it is okay to jump. Your subconscious which will only tell you the truth, will probably say, "No, don't jump; **it will probably kill you**." Pressure packed tennis matches can create similar interactions between your conscious and subconscious mind. By way of illustration, I will repeat the scenario described in chapter one. If you happen to find yourself in the Wimbledon singles final against the all-time great Roger Federer and you are serving and have reached match point for you, your nerves will surely be tested in this pressure-packed setting. At this moment, your conscious mind will ask your subconscious if it is okay to go ahead and win. Your subconscious mind, which will always tell you the truth will likely say this, "Roger is ranked number one in the world and you are number 216 and you've never beaten him before." At this moment, your pulse, blood pressure and breathing rate may start to increase and your conscious mind, since it is receiving no encouragement from the subconscious decides to take over. We now have a problem because your conscious mind does not know how to hit a 130 mph serve with topspin to the backhand or any other serve for that matter. Keep in mind that the conscious mind does not know how to play tennis. It was only involved the first time you tried to serve or hit a ground stroke. However, your subconscious mind which has been conditioned through years and years of **practice** can do this consistently. Repeated practice has programmed the subconscious mind to produce incredible tennis if the conscious mind will only stay out of the way. However, if the conscious mind, which wants to **win very badly decides to take over**. The result can easily be; **fault; double fault**; and after losing, one's blood pressure and heart rate will slowly return to normal and the subconscious mind can now relax. The problem is that the conscious mind does not know how to play tennis, or at least not very well. So then, how do we engage our subconscious mind at this pivotal moment of the match? The key is visualization. The night before your big match with Roger, you must create that future you've always dreamed and make your dream come true. You can prepare for peak performance by visualizing this moment: playing points with no errors, the crowd noise, hitting the winning shot, shaking Roger's hand, receiving the 5 million dollar check, and speaking to the media afterwards. You must do this with **total focus**, removing all negative thoughts. The next day when that moment arrives, and when your conscious mind asks your subconscious if it's okay to win, your subconscious which cannot differentiate between **fantasy and reality**, will tell you the truth. **"You beat him last night."**

Hydration and Sunscreen: Hydration is important in most sports, particularly tennis. Because tennis may be played under hot, humid conditions outdoors and has no time limit, hydration can be a huge factor in determining the winner of a match. One of the nice things about tennis is that you are given plenty opportunities to hydrate, since breaks are given between odd games. Tennis **coaches** should insure that their players have enough water to hydrate and a sports drink to replenish electrolytes and nutrients lost through sweating. If players don't stay hydrated, fatigue can set in early and impact a player's competitive will. Even though most players will probably supply their own sun protection, coaches should have **sunscreen available** for all players when playing outdoors.

Equipment: A coach bears the **primary responsibility** to ensure players are **properly equipped** to compete. The practicing of a positive outcome (visualization) the night before a big match **is not the only thing** necessary to play at one's full potential. You might think that a college player could make sure that their racquets are freshly strung. However, the reality is that **young busy** college athletes are not always prepared to play a grueling match. A coach should know that 12 players, (6 women and 6 men) need two identical racquets freshly strung with the same string and tensions before every match. **Two experienced stringers** and two stringing machines should be sufficient to accomplish this important task. This should be part of the tennis budget and these stringers should be given sufficient hours to keep every team member in freshly-strung racquets throughout the season. **Unsuitable stringing** is the most common way that college players can acquire an injury that will leave them unable to perform. Wrist and arm injuries caused by ill-suited racquet stringing can wreak havoc on a young player's future. Strings that are too tight or too stiff may wear well, but can be tough on young arms and cause serious injury requiring lengthy periods of rest and rehab. **Cost** may be the primary factor in string selection while the stress this choice puts on a young arm is undervalued.

Water and snacks should be in every player's racquet bag plus any other items that will ensure all players are properly hydrated and fueled. If the budget will allow, it is a good idea to allow for two days acclimation when traveling to an important championship. Different court surfaces, weather conditions and elevation changes need a period of adjustment in order to give team members every opportunity to play their best tennis.

Best Behavior: Before these important championships commence, the coach should remind players that they are representing their college or university and that everyone should be on their **best behavior**. This message needs **repeating** before, during and after the season.

You must be a Great Recruiter: Without great players, you won't have a great team. A coach should be an active recruiter by attending National Tournaments and junior practices where allowed.

Recommended Weekly Practice Schedule (Sample): Two hour practices; four days/week (off season) Division 1 teams allowed 20 hours/wk.

Monday – Primary focus; <u>challenge matches and tie-breaker round robins</u>

    Stretch and loosen up. (5 minutes)

    Matches (115 minutes) – 2 of 3 sets; tie-breaker for third

Tuesday – Primary focus; <u>serving, service return and transition play</u>

    Stretch and loosen up. (5 minutes)

    Jog the lines; refer to pp. 99-100 (Allow 5 minutes.)

    Serve – each player hits 60 serves, 30 ad court, and 30 deuce court. Changes ends after 30 serves (30 minutes)

    Transition play – two servers, one receiver; when server wins 3 points in a row, sever becomes receiver (90 minutes)

Wednesday – Primary focus; <u>finishing points, overheads, volleys; passing shots</u>

Stretch and loosen up. (5 minutes)

Jog the lines; refer to pp. 99-100 (Allow 5 minutes.)

Practice the following:

Overheads; use ball machines or players feeding (30 minutes)
Winning volleys; use ball machines if possible (25 minutes)

Passing shots together with winning volleys; emphasize clearing the net on all passing shots (30 minutes)

Drop shots, redrops and topspin lobs (25 minutes)

Thursday – Primary focus; doubles

    Stretch and loosen up. (5 minutes)

    Play doubles – experiment with different teams; emphasize poaching. (110 minutes)

    Run the Lines for Time. pp.99-100 (Allow 5 minutes.)

Injuries: Remember, a coach must do everything within reason to keep a college team **injury free.** That requires a constant **vigilance** of all drills and practice matches by the coach. Doing repetition (e. g. heavy hitting from the backcourt) in windy conditions should be avoided.

Loose tennis balls that are accidently **stepped on** while practicing. Sprained ankles and twisted knees can be the gruesome result. This can easily occur in windy conditions where balls are rolling around behind players who are focused on playing a point or hitting a shot.

Improper use of weights: Often time trainers who develop weight programs for sports that are focused on strength and power, will develop programs for tennis players that can be counterproductive. These programs should be closely evaluated by the coach in consultation with the college's trainers. **Agility drills** and **flexibility training** are excellent for improving the court coverage of **all** players. Service improvement and practicing shots that finish points are the best way for **quick** players to progress.

Excessive running: Agility drills such as jogging or running the lines should be the preferred types of conditioning. Distance running is to be avoided. Even a mile distance is of very little benefit in a sport that puts a premium on **flexibility and quickness.**

Fatherly Advice: My dad was a World War II veteran, who enlisted in both the Army and the Navy. He was also an athlete and a very good one. He loved football and played 4 years at Marshall University. He gave me this advice. "Son, play the sports you love and play them **smart** and **hard.** But remember this, if you become hurt and are unable to play, you are no longer an athlete, you are a **spectator.**"

Chapter 12
Professional

$\mathscr{F}$or the average sport's fan, professional tennis **team** competition can be thoroughly confusing. The Women's Tennis Association (WTA) has the Fed Cup, which in 2020 was renamed the **Billie Jean King Cup** in honor of the legendary Billie Jean King. [13] The men's game has three team competitions. The International Tennis Federation (ITF) runs the **Davis Cup**, which was named the Davis Cup in honor of an American tennis player Dwight Davis. Dwight donated the first trophy in 1900. The Association of Tennis Professionals (ATP) has the **ATP Cup.** Roger Federer wagered that the tennis equivalent of the Ryder Cup (An International golf competition held between the United States and Europe) would be a successful tennis event. Roger determined that since Europe had the most players ranked in the ATP top 100, the competition should be between Europe and the rest of the world. Federer named it the **Laver Cup** in honor of the Australian great Rod Laver.

With the **exception** of the Laver Cup, the coaches or captains of the other professional teams are generally ex-playing professionals with extensive tour experience. Their primary purpose is to select the players that will represent their respective countries. Team captains also decide who will play singles and doubles and in what order. The selection process can be tricky, since some top players may have to choose between an obligation to play for their country and a more lucrative tournament commitment.

[14] The player selection for the **Laver Cup** depends partially on player ranking. Each team consists of six players, three of which are chosen based on ATP rankings after the French Open. Three additional players are chosen by the team captain. In 2021, team Europe captained by Bjorn Borg had all six players ranked in the **top ten.** Team World captained by John McEnroe had **none.** Team players are listed below.

[15] **Laver Cup 2021 Teams:**

Team Europe – Captain: Bjorn Borg

Daniil Medvedev (Russia)
Stefanos Tsitsipas (Greece)
Alexander Zverev (Germany)
Andrey Rublev (Russia)
Matteo Berrettini (Italy)
Casper Ruud (Norway)

Team World – Captain: John McEnroe

Felix Auger-Aliassime (Canada)
Denis Shapovalov (Canada)
Diego Schwartzman (Argentina)
Reilly Opelka (USA)
John Isner (USA)
Nick Kyrgios (Australia)

[16] The winning team is awarded 1.5 million in prize money ($250,000 apiece) and the losing team is awarded $750,000 ($125,000 apiece). Players are also given participation fees based on ranking. In 2020, Rafael Nadal was awarded approximately 2 million in total. Team Europe has won all four Laver Cup competitions, and in 2021 defeated Team World 14-1.

The **role** of Laver Cup team captains John McEnroe and Bjorn Borg are mostly one of selecting the team and determining doubles matchups and schedules. Since players have their own coaches and trainers, Laver Cup captains seldom coach players in the traditional sense, but will act a cheerleaders and make sure all rules are followed.

Team captains of the **Billie Jean Cup, Davis Cup,** and **ATP Cup,** in addition to selecting team members, may oversee team practices, hotel accommodations and equipment issues. Players selected for these three **Cups** typically will all have their own coaches, who may or may not be there for the team competition. Rather than coach the players, the coaches (captains) should be active in the selection of doubles teams, and the order of match play. The surface that favors the home team should be selected by the coach. Practices should be organized in consultation with the players and all stretching and strength training should be done on an **individual basis**. A policy of keeping everyone healthy should be a **top priority.** The coach should be an active cheer leader and try to develop team **unity.**

Chapter 13
The Future of Tennis – Revisited

*M*any of the changes that were predicted in my first book; *The Modern Guide for Tennis Improvement* have already occurred and many others are underway. [17] Automated judging of line calls have eliminated most line umpires in the grand slams and in the majority of the ATP and WTA tournaments. Clay court tournaments, most notably the French Open, will probably be the **last** of the Grand Slams to utilize **Hawk-eye Live** or some other electronic technology to umpire line calls. Since clay courts leave a mark, the human eye is a good judge for making the correct call. However, once a chair umpire falls and seriously hurts themselves climbing in or out of their chair to make a line call, automated line calling will surely follow.

[17] The **Hawk-Eye Live** system has a margin of error of $\pm$ 3.6 mm, so the system is not perfect, but appears to have the stamp of approval of the majority of professional players. The system is currently expensive, so amateur tournaments will be last to implement electronic line calling. As of 2021, the cost is $25,000 (USD) per court, per tournament. The **Hawk-Eye Live** system makes instantaneous calls, whereas the regular **Hawk-Eye** system has a review when players request it. Novak Djokovic had this to say about automated line calls. "When it comes to people present on the court during a match, including line (judges), I really don't see a reason why every single tournament in this world, in this technological advanced era, would not have what we had during the Cincinnati/New York tournaments. I feel like we are all moving towards that, and sooner or later there is no reason to keep line-umpires." Former World No 5 Kevin Anderson told Tennis Majors. "The system works really, really well. I think it completely takes out any of the guesswork. That sort of automation is happening all across the world, in so many different industries. It does seem to make sense, especially during this time. I say probably (COVID-19 is) accelerating that, because it definitely reduces human interaction."

[18] The tennis industry wants and needs **to improve** and many depend on the teaching professional to guide them in the proper direction. The sport of tennis, while constantly evolving, has an obligation to both players and fans to also improve. In fact all aspects of the tennis industry want and need renovation. This **desire to improve** is the essence of the human condition and a rare constant in an ever-changing world. The vision for a better tennis tomorrow includes changes in rules, scoring and line calls. The idea of giving each player **one serve** in grand slams and amateur tennis is on the surface a radical change and is rarely discussed as of this writing. However, in the opinion of this author,

this **will happen** and accomplish the following goals; shortened matches for professionals; speeding up play; more action; and more spectacular shot-making. Spectators want to see rallies, artistry, variety and athleticism and this change will give smaller players more opportunities for success. [19] There is evidence that this has already begun. Started during the 2020 shutdown, UTS (Ultimate Tennis Showdown), co-owned by renowned French tennis coach Patrick Mouratoglou, is set to revolutionize tennis. The 2021 UTS edition will see players having only **one serve** and each match will consist of four eight-minute quarters. When Patrick was asked what was new in 2021, he said, "Very nice things. You'll be surprised, positively. We want to make this show more and more exciting, so we decided to get **rid of the first serve**, because our feeling is that we don't want too many aces and service winners. It's a **bit boring**. We want to have rallies and fun, so that's why we get rid of it." When Patrick was asked what the players thought of only one serve, he responded, "I think there are two types of players: players who count on their **serve** a lot, and players who consider that their service is **not an asset**. Those ones will be extremely happy. You have only one serve, but they don't mind. They just put the ball in play and then they start running, right? Then you have the players who really depend a lot on their serves, and of course for them it is more difficult, but I think it's great for them because it's going to make them work a lot on the ground strokes. It is going to push them to be better at what they are not the best at and it is going to be also a good experience to improve." Patrick goes on to say that the average age of people watching entire tennis matches is 61. People under 40 years of age watch very little tennis because it is too long and not very exciting. He claims that his under 21 UTS participants watch highlights, samples, but never entire matches. Patrick thinks that every sport needs to grow its fan base and any sport that doesn't is going to die. Mouratoglou wants to change that and bring on board the younger generation with a new, more exciting and shorter brand of tennis.

Here are some of the rule changes that were implemented in 2021.
- ✓ First player to win four games wins the set. Tie-Break at 3-3
- ✓ Still best of 5 Sets
- ✓ No-Ad Scoring
- ✓ Play all Let Serves
- ✓ Free Fan Movement at any time
- ✓ Live Electronic Line Calling
- ✓ Shot Clock Enforced
- ✓ Video Review
- ✓ Towel Racks
- ✓ Shorter Warm-ups (one minute)
- ✓ Courtside Coaching
- ✓ Net Cams for TV watching (front row seats for fans)
- ✓ One Medical Time-Out per player per match
- ✓ Timed Bathroom Breaks: Max 3 minutes

Mouratoglou said his goal of building a unique product to attract new and younger fans to the sport has been achieved and in its first year in 2020 the league was watched by more than 20 million people and broadcast in over 100 countries. "On the business side we're starting a capital-raise campaign because we want to go next level next year. And for that we need some investors," he added.

[20] In my first book, *A Modern Guide for Tennis Improvement*, I outlined many rule changes and the reasoning behind them. A blend of Patrick's ideas and **traditional** scoring was the result. The following will give the reader my vision for the future of tennis.

Using **traditional** scoring and allowing **one serve**, two minutes could be allowed for rest between odd games, helping players recover from the longer rallies and giving advertisers more air time and fans added time to take their seats. There will be no need for five-set matches. **All matches will be best of three**. Service holds and breaks will become less predictable and every point will have more value. Also, there will be fewer points where players will give a poor effort. *Hawk-eye* or other electronic devices will make **all line calls and there will be no challenges**. Scoring will be automatic and will occur at all pro level tournaments, not just at the Grand Slams. At the amateur level, low-cost, high-speed camera technology will make automatic line-calling feasible, eliminating cheating at the junior and college level. **Errant ball tosses** will count as faults and all **service lets** will be in play. From the amateur to the professional, from the juniors to the adults, **coaching** will undergo dramatic changes. Technology will transform the way in which professional and amateur players are coached. Electronic devices will be **allowed on court** and players will have access through an app that tracks all data. At both the professional and amateur levels, software systems like *PlaySight* will track all action on court. Winners, errors, ball placement and receiving positions will be collected and available for each player to view on the changeovers. **Since action will be electronically monitored**, data on the match can be accessed as the match progresses. In addition, players can receive texts from their coach and/or their team from anywhere in the world. There will be no need for a human coach on court. Players will also have access to the advice of **Artificial Intelligence (AI)** that will use this up-to-the-minute data to recommend the best strategy for players to follow. A **smart watch** using **AI** will be worn by all players that will recommend the best serves and the best returns to hit on all points. This is similar to what **good doubles teams** currently do after every point. The difference is that this advice will be coming from **AI** for singles players, instead of the advice coming from your doubles partner. Tennis will become primarily a game of **execution**.

Most tennis teaching professionals recognize that the **sport** of tennis is in need of **major improvements** if we want to grow the game and increase fan interest in professional tennis. The public is easily bored with five-hour professional tennis matches and 50 aces a match hit by seven footers. Currently, **tall** players are using their **considerable leverage** to hit 140+ mph serves to dominate with their power. The days of a Grand Slam champion under 6 feet tall appear to be over. Currently the Argentine Diego Swartzman is the only player in the ATP top twenty that is under **6 feet**. Most racquet sports allow only one serve; [21] **why is tennis different?** During the 16th and 17th centuries, when tennis was played primarily by the kings and queens of England and France, two serves were allowed and everyone served **underhand.** The net was higher and the court had different dimensions. The serve was only used to put the ball in play; not as an offensive weapon. In 1877 an English Club decided to hold a tennis championship on the lawns of what was known as the All England Croquet Club. The rules for that tournament were established by Englishman Dr. Henry Jones. Dr. Jones established the dimensions of the court, the scoring and the allowance of two serves. The reason for two serves was entirely one of tradition. It wasn't until 1880 that the net was lowered to three feet and that the overhead service was established as the norm for modern tennis. That **net height rule change** and **the two-serve rule** set by Englishman Dr. Henry Jones in 1880 have remained largely unchanged for 140 years.

Let us review the following questions and answers: **Why limit players to one serve?** One serve could accomplish the following; shorter matches, two of three sets for men and more opportunities for smaller players. **Why eliminate lines people?** High-speed cameras on all courts for both professional and amateur tournaments would eliminate challenges and curtail cheating at the amateur level. **Why play all let serves?** Let serves can be difficult to determine and would eliminate all controversies as to when a let serve occurs. The change to a no-let rule will create more fan interest and speed up some matches. Even though the no let rule is controversial, it is currently used in collegiate tennis and World Team Tennis (WTT).[22] WTT founder Billie Jean King has said that removing lets, "just makes for more drama." **Why penalize errant ball tosses?** Errant ball tosses are not only annoying to player and spectator alike, but would eliminate some trickery involved in disguising underhand serves. **Why eliminate ball boys and ball girls?** Replacing ball people with small ball retrieving robots will eliminate irregularities associated with ball gathering and lessen accidents to ball girls and ball boys retrieving balls. **Why eliminate the chair umpire?** Technology like *PlaySight* or similar technology will make all decisions and penalties involving bad behavior on court.

Toilet Breaks: [23] According to Article, Section W, Paragraph 4 of the 2021 Grand Slam Rule Book, women are limited to one toilet break per match (2 of 3 sets) and men are limited to two toilet breaks per match (3 of 5 set). These breaks should be "reasonable in length" and should allow for a change of clothes and/or a toilet break. In the 2021 first round match between Britian's Andy Murray and Greece's Stefanos Tsisipas. The match, which lasted 4 hours and 49 minutes, what constitutes "reasonable" was a point of contention between Andy Murray and the umpire. Stefanos did take over 8 minutes between the 4th and 5th set and this greatly upset Andy, who felt that it affected the outcome. This Grand Slam Rule needs to be reexamined and **changed**, so that both players know what to expect during match play. ESPN announcer 18 Grand Slam winner Chris Evert also felt the rule was too "vague". Chris went on to add that more than a five minute bathroom break gives a player time to read texts and possibly receive coaching. The USTA calls the pace of play an "important issue on our sport". The USTA wants to insure fairness and integrity in the sport of tennis. The WTA appears to be ready to change the rules when necessary. In defense of lengthy toilet breaks, some players claim that the need for hydration and profuse sweating in a closely contested match make these breaks necessary. **Changes** in the toilet breaks rules are coming and will make matches better for fans and players.

What about no-ad scoring? In my opinion, no-ad scoring has **no place** in the future of tennis. Colleges and the WTT currently use no-ad scoring and have been successful in shortening games at the expense of the excitement and unpredictability involved in long deuce games. The college game has embraced the no-ad rule change because it has made the length of head-to-head team match-ups shorter and hence more predictable. Although the no-ad rule shortens games, in both professional and amateur tennis it is **not** the games that need to be shortened, it's the **matches**. There might be a need for no-ad scoring in some junior tournaments in order to limit game length and help with scheduling. Adult amateur leagues might benefit from no-ad scoring for the same reasons.

Powerful serves and groundstrokes are the trademarks of the tall player: Because of their long arms and long legs, tall players are able to hit monster serves and generate more power off the ground than their smaller counterparts. [24] In an article written by Charlie Eccleshare that appeared on May 26, 2019 in "The Telegraph", Charlie discusses the emergence of the tall player in today's professional game. Without question, the giants of today's game, with their long legs and arms, are able to generate more power than their smaller counterparts. This article presents an excellent argument for the **one serve rule.** In the 2019 US Open 7 foot Reilly Opelka and 6 foot 10 inch John Isner hit a total of 81 aces in only three sets with no service breaks. If you do the math, that is 27 aces per set. The public's fascination with aces declines rapidly in matches that involve few service breaks. The aforementioned match drew few spectators in Louis Armstrong stadium despite the fact it was a close contest between two top Americans. Just as basketball fans quickly tire watching 7 footers dunk a basketball, tennis fans grow weary of the cascade of aces from the giants of the game. I repeat, **one serve instead of two** would speed up matches and make each point more valuable. Even if this rule change is made, tall players with big serves would still have a slight serving advantage over their smaller competitors, but the tall guys would be forced to compete more from the back of the court.

Smaller players like Spain's 5 foot 9 inch David Ferrer have voiced concern over the future dominance of these giants of the game. [25] A former number 3 in the world, Ferrer reflected on the game's future in 2015, "I think players like me, around my height, are going to be extinct." Only one player under 6 feet has won a grand since 2004. In that year the 5 foot 9 inch Argentine Gaston Gaudio won the French Open. In the years since the "big three" (Nadal, Federer, Djokovic), who are all over 6 feet (at least 6 foot 2 inches), have dominated the Grand Slams. But the future stars are all **much taller**. The 7 foot Reilly Opelka has said that the height of some of today's top players like Felix Aliassime (6 feet 4 inch), Daniil Medvedev (6 feet 6 inch) and Alexander Zverev (6 feet 6 inch) may become commonplace. Recent finalists in the US Open include 6 foot 8 inch South African Kevin Anderson, 6 foot 6 inch German Alexander Zevrev and 6 foot 6 inch Russian Daniill Medvedev. Anderson has also been a singles finalist at Wimbledon. These tall players represent only a portion of the giants of the men's game who are poised to dominate the future of men's professional tennis. The WTA also boasts its own share of tall female athletes. Maria Sharapova at 6 foot 2 inch and Venus Williams at 6 foot 1 inch are good examples. [26] Opelka observes this about the abundance of tall players in today's game. **"That's the new normal."** In the past, players who were Opelka's height were considered too slow and immobile to play top level tennis. But those disadvantages are now offset by the incredible power tall players are able to generate on the serve and forehand. Currently many tennis fans voice concern over the absence of smaller players in today's game. In the 60's 70's and 80's, tennis was dominated by players much smaller. The great champions of the past, Rod Laver, Bjorn Borg, Jimmy Connors and John McEnroe were all under 6 feet. In 1973, the average height of the world's top twenty players was 5 feet 9 inches. In 2020 the average height of the top twenty professionals is 6 feet 3 inches, with only three players in the top 20 that are shorter than 6 feet. Will this trend toward taller and taller players continue? Not if the **one serve** rule is adopted for all levels of play. The net is **low enough** and the service box **large enough** so that two serves are unnecessary.

If you happen to be a male and 6 feet 4 inches or taller, you probably have been asked, by complete strangers, this question: Do you play basketball? It is a recurrent question because basketball is recognized by the general public as a **tall man's** game. Tennis is poised to become the next tall man's game unless something is done to level the playing field for smaller players.

Bear in mind that the chapter you are reading is all about improving the game of tennis for the player and the fan. One thing you can't improve is your height. You can't coach height. You can't teach height. But you can improve your strength. You can improve your quickness. You can improve your racquet skills, but you can't change your height. For smaller players, this predicament is destined to be an **unachievable hurdle** for professional tennis advancement. With one serve the hurdle will be removed. The racquet sports of pickle ball, badminton, table tennis and squash all give the server just one serve: Why not tennis? If we put aside complaints from players and traditionalists for a moment, we can then just focus on how to achieve the one serve rule. In my opinion it must come from Wimbledon or from the great champions of the past. It was the first Wimbledon Championship in 1877 where the allowance of two serves was first established and I think the change must come from the same tournament that first established the rules. It might also come from the former champions of the 60's, 70's and 80's, who were all under 6 feet. After winning the Wimbledon boy's 18, Opelka has recently won his first ATP tournament. Even on the slow clay at Roland Garros, he remains a special talent that most players prefer to avoid. The 23 year-old Opelka has won over 90% of serves in his young career. The 6 foot 11 in Ivo Karlovic has combined his height and a great serve to stay a top contender for 20 years.

Spectators quickly tire of aces by tall players like Isner and Opelka and empty seats tend to be the norm. The average tennis fan cannot identify with aces hit by 7-footers. Nor can basketball fans connect with slam dunks by the giants of basketball. Tennis can and should bring back the smaller players along with their quickness, athleticism and shot making. The "one serve rule" would accomplish this and make for far more exciting tennis. To watch the great player Rafael Nada go through his various rituals and tics, hit a first serve fault, repeat rituals, hit a second serve let, repeat rituals and finally a third serve to put the ball in play contains no action and is a total waste of a minute and a half. I totally agree with Barry Glendenning who writes in the April 9th 2014 issue of **The Guardian** [27] "Despite assorted erudite opinions to the contrary, the argument for **abolishing the second serve** in tennis is fundamentally sound and remains compelling. The second serve rewards failure, wastes time and means we all have to spend far longer watching Rafael Nadal toweling his face, fiddling with his headband and pulling his shorts out from between his butt-cheeks than is necessary. The time has come to rid tennis of this superfluous second-serve menace. Alternatively, we could just keep it and eliminate the first serve instead." This author could not agree more. Studies have shown that less than 20% of a match time is spent with the ball in play. The Wall Street Journal (WSJ) timed the action in a recent Andy Murray match and found that there was only 26 minutes of play in a match that lasted two hours, 41 minutes. That's 16.4% of the match.[10] My own estimate is that a change to one serve would result in doubling the time that the ball is in play.

Why is the United State no longer the epicenter of professional tennis? A vibrant tennis **future** depends on **Retention!!!** The income the USTA receives from the US Open can easily fund grade school leagues and junior high tennis teams while promoting both varsity and JV tennis. The USTA push to promote "red ball, orange ball, green ball" will fade and should be replaced with fully-funded Grade School Leagues. **Greater funding should be given to challenger and futures events in the United States**. In addition, the USTA should work closely with the NCAA to **limit the number of foreign players** in college tennis to one per team. This will result in more opportunities for American players to play college tennis. Participation in junior tournaments (particularly the 16's and 18's) will increase once American juniors realize that they will have more chances to play tennis at the collegiate level.

Line calls: In the near future, technology will settle the majority of line calls at the **amateur and professional** level. Cameras installed on the net posts and the fences will video all points and will give players automatic scoring. Dual computer screens will be at the net posts and all line calls, foot faults and scoring will be automatic. Line umpires will be eliminated. *PlaySight* technology or similar will settle all disputes and will enforce the code of conduct. There will be no need for chair umpires. Young players who have grown up with cell phones, iPads and computers will readily accept these changes and trust them. All lines will be called by *Hawkeye* or other line calling innovations and scores will automatically be tallied by computer. No challenges will be allowed. Matches will flow smoothly and disputes between competitors will be minimized. If you consider the change that has occurred in bowling for example, when just 50 years ago, pins were reset by human pin setters and scoring was done with pencil and paper by the participating players. Today automatic pin setters and computer scoring have been installed which now create a more enjoyable atmosphere for participants.

Smart watches will monitor metabolic changes which will include blood pressure, heart rate, insulin decreases and hydration levels during matches to help players make nutrition decisions during changeovers. As mentioned earlier, they will also contain recommendations from AI for tactical changes as the match is happening.

[28] In the fall of **2015 Novak Djokovic** caught a glimpse into the **future** of tennis teaching. When Novak showed up in a posh section of northern New Jersey, the future of tennis teaching had **already arrived**. A forty million dollar compound, hidden behind partitioned gates, unveiled a forty acre wooded estate complete with a lake, numerous homes and manicured gardens. The property was put together by Robert Zoeller and his wife Victoria, but it was Robert's son, Gordon A. Uehling III, who had transformed a hillside stretch of this property into a high tech tennis world like no other. This parcel of land contained a Har-Tru court, a red clay court (the same red brick dust used in The French Open), a DecoTurf hard court (US Open surface) and a nearly completed grass court. [29] The show court however, was an indoor court equipped with a *PlaySight* Smart Court system of cameras that videos and tracks every shot and movement that a tennis player makes. PlaySight calls the lines, measures ball speed, spin and trajectory, point patterns, the distance a player covers and calories burned. On a courtside kiosk, all this information can be made available to both coach and student. Coach and student then analyze the captured data, plot a plan of action and note progress over weeks, months and even years. It should be noted that Novak Djokovic won his second US Open Singles title in 2015 with a 6-4, 5-7, 6-4, 6-4 victory over Roger Federer.

It was on this property in 2015 that Gordon first introduced Novak to the **CVAC hypobaric chamber**. [30] This egg-shaped pod simulates pressures at different altitudes and stimulates muscles by cyclical compression. This one hundred thousand dollar machine is great for recovery after a hard workout and increases one's red cell blood count. **CVAC** is the acronym for Cyclic Variations in Adaptive Conditioning. The hypobaric (less than normal air pressure) chamber differs from the hyperbaric (greater than normal air pressure) chamber in the following ways. The CVAC chamber operates with a sophisticated pressure controlled pumping system that is able to make rapid pressure changes that range from sea level to 22,500 feet. The CVAC system continually circulates outside air and forces the body to adapt to rapid pressure changes. While in the pod, your body will experience an oxygen debt which will activate the production of a hormone call erythropoietin. This protein is what stimulates the production of red blood cells. In roughly 20 minutes your body will achieve the following **benefits**: stamina and energy improvement; endurance should increase; inflammation and swelling will be reduced; improved sleeping patterns; improvement in mental acuity and alertness. The Englishman Roger Bannister (first man to break the four-minute mile) predicted that coaches would eventually use low-pressure chambers to train athletes artificially.

Standard hyperbaric chambers use oxygen to produce pressure variations between 8,000 and 10,000 feet. In a typical hyperbaric chamber there is no outside air that circulates inside the pod, since pressure changes are caused by oxygen variations. Additionally, hyperbaric sessions can take up to eight hours. **Hypobaric** sessions last less than ½ hour. If you can't afford to purchase the CVAC pod, hypobaric therapy sessions can be scheduled at many US sport training facilities.

Gordon Uehling III has since expanded his futuristic high tech teaching and as of 2020 owns and operates two tennis clubs in New Jersey that implement the *PlaySight* Smart Court system. The *PlaySight* system has been installed on all 15 indoor courts and has combined the talents of 24 teaching professionals to offer what I think is the most advanced tennis training system in the world. Gordon is the founder and owner of *CourtSense* training systems. He and his staff train not only adults and professionals but also children as young as three. Gordon's mission statement is to tap into the energy and spirit of each student by providing the finest in facilities, technologies and integrated tennis systems.

[31] The real **innovation** of *CourtSense* is found in the training of the staff. Each of the 24 teaching professionals are trained with an online proprietary coaching platform that gives detailed progressions, theories and the latest in sports science to help students **improve** and to **enjoy** the great game of tennis. This online training platform of all staff creates a cohesive team that can employ exceptional innovation in the coaching of all ages and abilities. It is this **unified** approach from dedicated and qualified tennis professionals and the *PlaySight* Smart Court system that make the *CourtSense* method of coaching unique.

Professionals who have trained extensively in this system include former WTA world-ranked #24 Christina McHale and former WTA world ranked #68 Bernarda Pera. Also, large numbers of highly-ranked juniors are in the pipeline that appear to be headed toward a future in professional tennis. It should be noted that this method is being implemented with great success in the coaching of **adult** players. There are instructional-based, match-based and fitness-based programs that can be practiced in private, semi-private or clinic settings. It is the opinion of the author that *CourtSense* offers a clear view of the future of tennis coaching.

[32] The **future of tennis** includes **online** tennis instruction. A powerful online method is available now and can be accessed at https://www.onlinetennisinstruction.com. Founder **Florian Meier** has created a world-renowned system that is based on current science and has had proven results with players of all levels and ages. His biomechanically sound methods are the **best available** online. He combines both experience and passion to produce hundreds of online videos that will guide any player through the **improvement** process. Florian and his team specialize in fixing weak serves, forehands and backhands with German precision. Florian is an USPTA certified professional with a MBA in Sports Management from San Diego State University. He currently has 100,000 online subscribers and many testimonials that testify to the efficacy of his methods. I **highly recommend Florian** and his modern approach to online tennis instruction.

The tennis community has a vested interest in keeping tennis growing and healthy. This means that tennis professionals, coaches and parents of tennis-playing children must create a tennis future that makes tennis more exciting for all ages, particularly the young. If the young are not excited about playing and watching tennis, the sport will eventually wither and die. At the moment 30 year olds and younger tennis players do not watch tennis matches in their entirety. They will watch highlights and short samples, but not much else. Why? Because tennis matches are too long (particularly men's matches) and rely too much on serves to win points and matches. The need of a vibrant future in tennis is obvious and rule changes must be made. There are two obvious rule changes that should be made in order to make tennis more exciting and allow men's and women's matches to play under the same rules. They are: **Eliminate the second serve** and require **2 of 3 sets for both men and women.** Tennis players at all levels do not need two serves to put the ball in play. **Two of three sets for both men and women will eliminate the argument that men should be paid more because they play 3 of 5.** Presently at all levels of play, 70% of all points last 4 shots or less and the majority of points last 2 shots or less. Players and fans want more tennis; not wasted time between points. Giving players **one serve** will easily accomplish what younger players and fans want. So then what do they want? They want **more tennis and shorter matches.** Tennis fans and the younger generation are tired of tall guys hitting aces and unreturnable serves for four or five hours. Fans want shorter matches; not shorter games; not shorter sets, but shorter matches. Everyone wants less brow wiping, less ball bouncing and fewer errant ball tosses. Tennis can and **must change** or the dazzling sport of tennis will have **no future.** Tennis fans **don't mind** long points or long games; in fact most fans enjoy the long points and long games that traditional scoring offers. What they **don't want is longer matches**. We must give them what they want or risk losing the tennis fan base to other sports that are more fan-centric.

Periodically, **a rare exception** to the above shortened match format **(one serve and 2of 3 sets for men)** has occurred. The 2022 Australian Open Final between Spain's Rafael Nadal and Russia's Danil Medvedev was a prime example of this exception. This drama-filled 5 hour and 24 minute match was won by Nadal by the score of 2-6, 6-7, 6-4, 6-4, 7-5. It was the second longest match in Australian Open history and moved Nadal ahead of his two rivals (Roger Federer and Novak Djokovic) in the list of Grand Slam winners. This amazing match was an incredible performance of athleticism, artistry, grit, emotion and endurance and was displayed by both players, who were playing at the highest level of professional tennis. The **entertainment value** was beyond belief. After the match, Nadal admitted that it was the greatest comeback of his career and one of the most emotional.

However, I do believe that the **two rule changes** I have suggested **will** happen and succeed in reducing the length of long matches in men's tennis and will make the game more exciting for both the spectator and the participant. We must restore the **artistry** that has made tennis a popular sport worldwide. With the help of **tennis professionals**, **coaches** and **invested parents**, these two changes will ensure a **bright future** for our **beautiful game of tennis.**

Citations

Foreword

[1] Author Unknown (2020), National Tennis Organizations and Associations. Do It Tennis.
https://www.doittennis.com/knowledge-center/tennis-organizations

Chapter 1

[2] Vercelletto, Niko (Dec 2, 2021) catching up with Rick Macci: Working with Serena and Venus Williams and evolving his coaching Style. Retrieved from
https://www.tennis.com/baseline/articles/catching-up-with-rick-macci-working-with-serena-and-venus-williams-coaching

[3] WTA editors (April 22, 2020), One-Handed Backhands. Retrieved from https://www.wtatennis.com/photos/1655885/single-stars-the-highest-ranked-one-handed-backhands-on-tour

[4] Jonathon Braden (June 3, 2019), Federer Leads the Way, but Thiem, Tsitsipas Carry on the One-Handed Backhand. Retrieved

from https://www.atptour.com/en/news/federer-tsitsipas-future-one-handed-backhand-2019

[5] Harvey Fialkov (December 18, 2021), *Unorthodox style gives junior tennis sensation from Bulgaria problems for opponents. Miami Herald.* Retrieved from https://www.miamiherald.com/sports/article256685522.html

[6] Johnathan Swan (August 17, 2019*), Hybrid Stringing - Roger Federer's Stringing Method of Choice.* peRFect Tennis. Retrieved from https://www.perfect-tennis.com/hybrid-stringing/

[7] Williams, J. R. (2020). p 60, *A Modern Guide for Tennis Improvement.* Amazon KDP Publishing

Chapter 5

[8] Williams, J. R. (2020). pp 41-45, *A Modern Guide for Tennis Improvement.* Amazon KDP Publishing

[9] Agence France-Presse (January 11, 2022) Sabalenka's Serve Melts Down In Australian Open Warm-Up Disaster. Retrieved from https://sports.ndtv.com/tennis/21-double-faults-world-no-2-aryna-sabalenkas-serve-melts-down-in-australian-open-warm-up-disaster-2701820

[10] Nick Braven (January 11, 2020) Aryna Sabalenka made 39 double faults in 2 matches in 2022. Retrieved from https://thetennistime.com/aryna-sabalenka-made-39-double-faults-in-2-matches-in-2022/

Chapter 11

[11] Tom FitzGerald (February 2, 2018) In 57 years of Stanford tennis, Dick Gould delivered aces. Retrieved from https://www.sfgate.com/collegesports/article/In-57-years-of-Stanford-tennis-Dick-Gould-12547947.php

[12] The New York Times Archives (May 30, 1978). Retrieved from https://www.nytimes.com/1978/05/30/archives/sports-news-briefs-mcenroe-defeats-sadri-for-ncaa-net-title-loss-in.html

Chapter 12

[13] Vijay Krishnamurthy (January 2, 2020) The Tale of 3 Cups – Davis, Laver and ATP. Retrieved from https://www.sportskeeda.com/tennis/the-tale-of-3-cups-davis-laver-and-atp

[14] Christopher Clarey (October 4, 2021) At the Laver Cup, Europe Might Be Too Good. Retrieved from https://www.nytimes.com/2021/09/27/sports/tennis/laver-cup-europe-world.html

[15] Risa, M. (September 22, 2021) Laver Cup 2021 Teams, Rules and Format. Retrieved from https://surprisesports.com/tennis/laver-cup-2021-teams/

[16] Author unknown (September 21, 2021) Laver Cup 2021 Prize Money Breakdown: How Much Will the Winning Team and Each Tennis Player Earn? Retrieved from https://www.essentiallysports.com/atp-tennis-news-laver-cup-2021-prize-money-breakdown-how-much-will-the-winning-team-and-each-tennis-player-earn/

Chapter 13

[17] Shahid Judge (February 3, 2021), Explained: How Hawk-eye Live is replacing line-officials and decongesting tennis courts in COVID times. Retrieved from https://indianexpress.com/article/explained/hawk-eye-live-tennis-coronavirus-7171229/

[18] Williams, J. R. (March, 2021), Tennis Improvements. *Addvantage Magazine.* pp 58-59.

[19] Mouratoglou, Patrick (May 24, 2021), Interview. Retrieved from https://www.tennismajors.com/uts-actualite/patrick-mouratoglou-uts4-rules-format-fans-serve-younger-generation-instagram-408540.html

[20] Williams, J. R. (2020). pp 103-119, *A Modern Guide for Tennis Improvement.* Amazon KDP Publishing

[21] Linder, B. (July 9, 2018), Today in History: *The first Wimbledon tournament begins.* Roodepoort record. https://roodepoortrecord.co.za/2018/07/09/today-in-history-the-first-wimbledon-tournament-begins-web/

[22] Rothenberg, Ben (January 19, 2013), *Do-Over Serves Are Eliminated in an Experiment on a Lower ATP Tour.* Retrieved from https://www.nytimes.com/2013/01/20/sports/tennis/tennis-trying-a-no-let-experiment-on-serves.html

[23] Howard Fendrich (August 31, 2012) Bathroom stall: Tennis toilet break talk swirls in Flush-ing. Retrieved from https://sports.yahoo.com/bathroom-stall-tennis-toilet-break-212204631.html

[24] Eccleshare, C. (May 26, 2019), Special Report: *With their long levers and easy power men's tennis is becoming the land of the giants.* The Telegraph UK. https://www.telegraph.co.uk/tennis/2019/05/26/long-levers-easy-power-mens-tennis-becoming-land-giants/

[25] Vallejo, J. J. (2015), *David Ferrer: Tennis' Small Wonder on Keeping the Big Guys at Bay.* Rolling Stone. https://www.rollingstone.com/culture/culture-sports/david-ferrer-tennis-small-wonder-on-keeping-the-big-guys-at-bay-89092/

[26] Flink, S. (October 3, 2018), *American Reilly Opelks Stands Tall Going Into The 2019 Season.* Tennis. https://www.tennis.com/pro-game/2018/10/reilly-opelka-exclusive-interview-american-tennis/77327/

[27] Glenndenning, B. (April 9, 2014), *Breaking the Law: abolish the second serve from tennis.* The Guardian. https://www.theguardian.com/sport/blog/2014/apr/09/breaking-the-law-abolish-tennis-second-serve

[28] Marzorati, G. (August 28, 2015), *The World's Most High-Tech Tennis Coach.* The New Yorker. https://www.newyorker.com/sports/sporting-scene/tennis-2-0

[29] Author Unknown (2020), Play Sight. My Play Sight. https://my.playsight.com/#/

[30] Author Unknown (2020), *CVAC Hypobaric Chamber.* Beverly Hills Rejuvenation Center.

[31] Retrieve from https://www.courtsense.com/courtsense-staff/

[32] Retrieved from https://www.onlinetennisinstruction.com/